The Everyday Chef

PASTA
AND RICE

Published by Celebrity Press
An imprint of Hambleton-Hill Publishing, Inc.
Nashville, Tennessee 37218

Printed and bound in the United States of America

ISBN 1-58029-015-9

10 9 8 7 6 5 4 3 2 1

Graphic Design/Art Direction
John Laughlin

Contents

Conversion Table 4

Pasta with Meat 5

Pasta with Seafood 11

Pasta with Chicken 17

Pasta with Vegetables 23

Pasta Salads 31

Ethnic Dishes 37

Pasta Classics 45

Rice Dishes 53

Index 64

Conversion Table

Metric Conversions

1/8 teaspoon = .05 ml
1/4 teaspoon = 1 ml
1/2 teaspoon = 2 ml
1 teaspoon = 5 ml
1 tablespoon = 3 teaspoons = 15 ml
1/8 cup = 1 fluid ounce = 30 ml
1/4 cup = 2 fluid ounces = 60 ml
1/3 cup = 3 fluid ounces = 90 ml
1/2 cup = 4 fluid ounces = 120 ml
2/3 cup = 5 fluid ounces = 150 ml

3/4 cup = 6 fluid ounces = 180 ml
1 cup = 8 fluid ounces = 240 ml
2 cups = 1 pint = 480 ml
2 pints = 1 liter
1 quart = 1 liter
1/2 inch = 1.25 centimeters
1 inch = 2.5 centimeters
1 ounce = 30 grams
1 pound = 0.5 kilogram

Oven Temperatures

Fahrenheit	Celsius
250°F	120°C
275°F	140°C
300°F	150°C
325°F	160°C
350°F	180°C
375°F	190°C
400°F	200°C
425°F	220°C
450°F	230°C

Baking Dish Sizes

American	Metric
8-inch round baking dish	20-centimeter dish
9-inch round baking dish	23-centimeter dish
11 x 7 x 2-inch baking dish	28 x 18 x 4-centimeter dish
12 x 8 x 2-inch baking dish	30 x 19 x 5-centimeter dish
9 x 5 x 3-inch baking dish	23 x 13 x 6-centimeter dish
1 1/2-quart casserole	1.5-liter casserole
2-quart casserole	2-liter casserole

Pasta with Meat

Al dente:
An Italian term meaning "firm to the teeth."

Blue Cheese:
A rich, blue-veined cheese, similar to Roquefort.

Creamy Ham Rotini Bake

2 c. fresh broccoli florets
1 1/2 c. Cheddar cheese, shredded
1 1/2 c. ham, coarsely chopped
1 1/2 c. Rotini, cooked and drained
1/2 c. salad dressing
1/2 green pepper, chopped
1/4 c. milk

Preheat oven to 350°F. Stir together all ingredients except 1/2 cup cheese. Pour into 1 1/2-quart casserole. Sprinkle with remaining 1/2 cup cheese. Bake for 30 minutes or until thoroughly heated.

Easy Pasta

1 lb. ground beef
1 jar spaghetti sauce
1/2 c. Parmesan cheese, grated
5 c. pasta, cooked
2 c. mozzarella cheese, shredded

Preheat oven to 375°F. Meanwhile, brown ground beef in skillet; drain. Add spaghetti sauce, Parmesan cheese, and pasta. Spoon into 13x9-inch baking dish. Top with mozzarella cheese. Bake for 20 minutes.

Cheeseburger Macaroni

1/2 lb. ground beef
2 1/4 c. water
1/2 c. catsup
1 tsp. mustard
1 7-oz. pkg. elbow macaroni
3/4 lb. processed cheese, cubed

Brown meat in large skillet; drain. Stir in water, catsup, and mustard. Bring to boil. Add macaroni. Reduce heat to medium-low. Cover and simmer 8 to 10 minutes or until macaroni is tender. Remove from heat and add cheese. Stir until melted.

Sausage Lasagna Rolls

1 12-oz. pkg. turkey sausage
1 c. ricotta cheese
1 c. mozzarella cheese
1/3 c. Parmesan cheese, grated
1 tsp. dried Italian seasoning
6 lasagna noodles, cooked and drained
1 15-oz. can Italian-style tomato sauce

Break sausage into small pieces; fry in skillet on medium-high heat, 10 minutes or until lightly browned. Add cheeses and Italian seasoning. Spread about 1/2 cup sausage mixture on each lasagna noodle and roll tightly. Put lasagna rolls seam-side down in microwaveable baking dish and top with tomato sauce. Cover and microwave on high power for 12 minutes, rotating dish halfway through heating.

Bacon and Cream Cheese Pasta

1 pkg. bacon, cut into 1/2-inch pieces
1 c. mushrooms, sliced
2 green onions, sliced
8 oz. medium egg noodles, uncooked
1 8-oz. pkg. cream cheese, cubed
2/3 c. milk
1/2 tsp. garlic powder
1/2 tsp. dried basil
1/2 tsp. dried thyme leaves
1 small tomato, chopped

Cook bacon until crisp. Stir in mushrooms and onions. Cook, stirring constantly, for 4 minutes. Prepare pasta according to package directions; drain. Return noodles to saucepan and add all remaining ingredients except tomato. Cook and stir on medium heat until cheese melts. Toss bacon mixture with noodles. Top with tomato and serve.

Beef 'n Macaroni

1 lb. ground beef
1/2 c. onion, chopped
1 15-oz. can tomato sauce
3/4 c. Parmesan cheese, grated and divided
1/2 tsp. dried basil leaves, crushed
1 pkg. macaroni and cheese dinner
2 tbsp. butter or margarine
2 tbsp. flour
1 1/2 c. milk
2 eggs, beaten

Preheat oven to 350°F. Brown meat and drain. Stir in onion and cook until tender. Add tomato sauce, 1/2 cup Parmesan cheese, and basil. Simmer for 10 minutes, stirring occasionally. Prepare macaroni and cheese dinner according to package directions. Spread meat mixture onto bottom of 9-inch square baking dish. Top with macaroni dinner. Melt butter in saucepan on low heat. Blend in flour. Gradually add milk and cook, stirring constantly, until thickened. Stir small amount of hot mixture into eggs, then return to hot mixture. Pour hot mixture over dinner and sprinkle with remaining 1/4 cup Parmesan cheese. Bake for 45 to 50 minutes or until golden brown.

Inside-Out Calzone

1 lb. ground beef
garlic and oregano to taste
2 oz. pepperoni, sliced
1 pkg. radiatore pasta
2 c. mozzarella cheese, grated
2 lb. ricotta cheese
1 small can tomato sauce

Preheat oven to 350°F. Brown meat, spices, and pepperoni. Boil water and cook pasta until *al dente*. Mix meat and cheese in a large pan; add cooked pasta. Spread evenly throughout pan. Drizzle tomato sauce on top and bake for 20 to 30 minutes, or until cheese is just starting to turn brown.

Pasta and Pork Stir-Fry

1 lb. linguine
1 tbsp. sesame oil
2 garlic cloves, minced
4 c. cabbage, thinly sliced
1 c. green onions with tops, thinly sliced
1 1/2 c. red bell pepper, thinly sliced
1 medium carrot, shredded
1/2 tsp. salt
1/2 tsp. red pepper flakes
1 1/2 c. pork tenderloin, cut into thin strips

Prepare pasta according to package directions; drain. Meanwhile, heat oil in large skillet. Stir in all ingredients except pork and linguine.

Stir-fry until tender. Add meat and lightly stir-fry until cooked. Add hot linguine; toss to mix. Serve immediately.

Sausage Spaghetti

3 slices bacon, chopped
2 Italian sausages, casings removed
1 pkg. spaghetti noodles
2 eggs, beaten
3 tbsp. Parmesan cheese

Brown bacon and sausage. Meanwhile, cook pasta according to package directions; drain and rinse. Put noodles back in pot.

Stir in bacon, sausage, beaten eggs, and Parmesan cheese. Toss to mix well. Serve with salad and garlic or cheese bread.

Chorizo Noodle Casserole

12 oz. Rotini
1 tbsp. butter
4 medium-size chorizo sausages
1 small onion, chopped coarse
1 can (4 oz.) green chilies, chopped
1 c. milk
1/2 tsp. salt
1 dash pepper
2 c. Monterey Jack cheese, shredded
6 to 8 tomato slices

Following package directions, cook Rotini in a large kettle of boiling, salted water until *al dente*. Drain, rinse with cold water, and drain again. Meanwhile, melt butter in a wide frying pan over medium-high heat. Remove sausage casings, crumble meat into pan, add onion, and cook until sausage is browned and onion is limp (about 5 minutes). Pour off drippings and add cooked pasta, chilies, milk, salt, and pepper to taste.

Pour half of mixture into a greased 2 1/2-quart casserole; sprinkle with half of cheese. Add remaining mixture, arrange tomato slices on top, and sprinkle with remaining cheese. If made ahead, cover and refrigerate until next day. Bake, uncovered, in a 350°F oven for 25-35 minutes or until top is slightly browned.

Fettuccine With Peas and Ham

5 tbsp. unsalted butter
6 green onions
8 oz. mushrooms, sliced
1 1/4 c. whipping cream
1 pkg. (10 oz.) frozen tiny peas
4 oz. boiled ham, chopped
1 c. Parmesan cheese
1 lb. fettuccine, cooked
salt and pepper to taste

Melt butter in heavy skillet over medium heat. Add onions and sauté until soft. Add mushrooms,

increase heat to high and cook until mushrooms are very lightly browned. Add cream and boil two minutes. Stir in peas and cook about 30 seconds. Reduce heat to low; blend in ham, cheese and fettuccine and toss until heated, well combined, and sauce clings to pasta. Season to taste. Serve immediately.

Ham and Asparagus Pasta

2 cans (14-1/2-oz. ea.) stewed tomatoes, cut up
1 tbsp. dried parsley flakes
1/2 tsp. dried basil, crushed
1/2 tsp. dried oregano, crushed
1/8 tsp. ground red pepper (optional)
1 c. evaporated skim milk
10 oz. multi-colored pasta such as wagon
   wheel or corkscrew
3/4 lb. fresh asparagus spears, woody bases
   snapped off and discarded and bias-sliced
   into 1-inch pieces; *or* 10 oz. frozen
   asparagus, thawed and drained
6 oz. lean ham, fully cooked and cut into
   bite-sized strips
1 small red or green sweet pepper,
   cut into strips
grated Parmesan cheese (optional)

In a medium saucepan combine stewed tomatoes, parsley, basil, oregano, and ground red pepper, if using. Bring to boiling. Simmer sauce, uncovered, about 15 minutes or until reduced to 2 1/2 cups, stirring occasionally. Add evaporated milk all at once, stirring constantly. Heat mixture through; do not boil.

Meanwhile, prepare pasta according to package directions. During last 4 minutes of cooking time, add asparagus, ham, and sweet pepper to the boiling water. Cook 4 minutes. Drain pasta and vegetables. Place pasta mixture on a serving platter. Spoon sauce over pasta. Serve with Parmesan cheese, if desired. Serve at once.

Italian Sausage Fettucine

2 tbsp. butter
2 tbsp. flour
2 c. milk
7 hot Italian sausage links
1 large onion, chopped
pinch cayenne pepper
1 tbsp. garlic powder
2 tbsp. parsley flakes
salt to taste
1/2 tsp. black pepper

Make a white sauce with butter, flour, and milk. Set aside.

Squeeze meat from sausage casings and fry. Add onion and continue cooking until onions are translucent and sausage meat is completely cooked. Add garlic powder, parsley, salt, pepper, and cayenne to sausage mixture. Mix thoroughly.

Meanwhile, begin boiling water for fettucine. Add white sauce to meat mixture in frying pan and simmer while fettucine is cooking. When fettucine is *al dente*, drain and rinse in hot water. Serve by ladling meat and sauce mixture over top of hot fettucine.

Pasta With Tomatoes, White Beans, and Pepperoni

1 garlic clove, sliced thinly
1 tbsp. olive oil
1/4 c. onion, chopped
1/3 c. pepperoni, chopped coarse
16 oz. plum tomatoes with juice, chopped
1/2 tsp. basil, crumbled
1/4 tsp. oregano, crumbled
1/4 tsp. hot red pepper flakes
salt and pepper to taste
2/3 c. canned white beans, drained and rinsed well
1 tbsp. fresh parsley, minced
1/4 lb. tubular pasta
Parmesan cheese, grated

In a heavy skillet, cook garlic in oil over moderate heat until golden, stirring constantly. Remove with a slotted spoon and discard. Add onion and pepperoni to oil and cook over medium-low heat, stirring occasionally, for 3 minutes. Add tomatoes with juice, basil, oregano, pepper flakes, and salt and pepper to taste. Simmer, stirring occasionally, for 5 minutes. Add beans and parsley and continue simmering, partially covered, for 5-7 minutes or until slightly thickened. Cook pasta in boiling salted water until *al dente*; drain well. In a bowl, toss pasta with sauce. Divide pasta between 2 heated bowls. Sprinkle with Parmesan cheese and garnish with parsley sprigs. Serve.

Polish Reuben Casserole

2 cans (10 3/4 oz. ea.) condensed cream
  of mushroom soup
1 1/3 c. milk
1/2 c. onion, chopped
1 tbsp. prepared mustard
2 cans (16 oz. ea.) sauerkraut,
  rinsed and drained
1 pkg. (8 oz.) medium-width noodles
1 1/2 lb. Polish sausage, fully cooked
  and cut into 1/2-inch pieces
2 c. (8 oz.) Swiss cheese, shredded
3/4 c. whole wheat bread crumbs
2 tbsp. butter, melted

Combine soup, milk, onion and mustard in medium bowl; blend well. Spread sauerkraut in a greased 13x9-inch pan. Top with uncooked noodles. Spoon soup mixture evenly over top. Top with sausage, then cheese. Combine crumbs and butter in small bowl; sprinkle over top. Cover pan tightly with foil. Bake at 350° F for 1 hour or until noodles are tender. Garnish as desired.

Pierogi With Meat

2 c. leftover meat pieces
2 slices wet bread, squeezed
1 onion, chopped
1 tbsp. bacon drippings
salt and pepper to taste
3 slices bacon, diced
1 egg
3 1/4 c. flour
pinch salt
1/2 c. water
1 1/2 tbsp. butter, melted
1 1/2 tbsp. bread crumbs

For stuffing, grind meat with bread. Sauté onions in bacon drippings; add to bread. Season with salt and pepper.

For dough, mix egg with flour, dash of salt, and as much water as needed to knead a smooth, loose dough. Roll out thin. Cut out 2 1/2-3-inch squares. Put a small amount of stuffing on each square. Fold to form a triangle; pinch edges together. Cook in boiling salted water on high heat for 5 minutes. Remove to a warmed serving platter.

Add bread crumbs to butter and fry for a few minutes over low heat. Pour over pierogi.

Rigatoni With Sausage

1 lb Italian sausage, casings removed
1 clove garlic, minced
2 c. spaghetti sauce
1/4 c. dry red wine *or* water
1/4 c. mild peppers, sliced and drained
1/2 c. olives, quartered
1 c. cheese, grated
4 c. rigatoni, cooked and hot

In 10-quart skillet over medium heat, cook sausage until browned, stirring to separate meat. Spoon off fat. Add garlic, sauce, wine or water, and peppers. Heat to boiling. Reduce heat to low; simmer 5 minutes, stirring occasionally. Add olives, 1/2 cup cheese and rigatoni; toss to coat well. Top with remaining cheese and serve.

Swiss Spaghetti

4 tsp. butter
1 medium onion, chopped
1 green pepper, chopped
1 lb. ground beef
2 c. canned tomatoes
1 1/2 tsp. salt
1/2 tsp. pepper
3/4 lb. Swiss cheese, cubed
1 lb. spaghetti, cooked
1/2 c. Swiss cheese, grated

In saucepan, melt butter and sauté onion and green pepper for about 5 minutes. Add beef and cook over high heat until browned. Add tomatoes, salt and pepper. Cover and simmer 1 hour. Add cubed cheese and cook 5 minutes. Add spaghetti and toss. Serve with grated cheese.

Quick Baked Pasta

2 tbsp. olive oil
1 lb. ground beef, lean
2 cloves garlic, crushed
1/2 c. half-and-half
3/4 c. marinara sauce
3/4 lb. penne pasta
1/4 c. Parmesan cheese, grated
1 tsp. dried oregano
1/2 tsp. dried rosemary
salt and pepper to taste
1 c. mozzarella or Swiss cheese, grated

Heat a large frying pan. Add oil, beef, and garlic. Sauté until meat is tender; drain excess fat. Add all remaining ingredients except mozzarella cheese and pasta. Let simmer while cooking pasta. Cook pasta in 4 quarts boiling water until *al dente*. Drain and mix with sauce. Pour into a 3-quart baking dish and top with remaining cheese. Bake, uncovered, at 350°F for 25 minutes or until hot and bubbling.

Pasta with Seafood

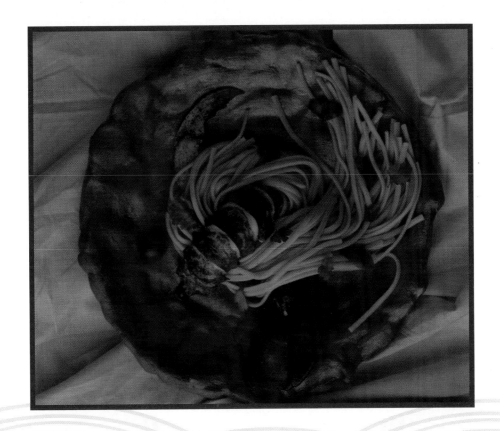

Chop:
To cut into small, irregular-shaped pieces.

Combine:
To stir together two or more ingredients.

Tuna Pasta Salad

1/2 lb. Rotini
1 12 1/2-oz. can tuna, drained
2 c. cucumbers, thinly sliced
1 tomato, chopped
1/2 c. celery, sliced
1/4 c. green pepper, chopped
1/4 c. green onions, sliced
1 c. Italian dressing
1/4 c. mayonnaise
1 tbsp. prepared mustard
1 tsp. dill weed
1 tsp. salt
1/8 tsp. ground black pepper

Prepare Rotini according to package directions; drain. In a large bowl combine prepared Rotini, tuna, cucumbers, tomato, celery, green pepper, and onions. Blend Italian dressing, mayonnaise, mustard, and seasonings in a small bowl; toss with salad mixture. Cover and chill two hours or overnight before serving.

Linguine Tuna Salad

7 oz. linguine, broken in half
1/4 c. lemon juice
1/4 c. vegetable oil
1/4 c. green onions, chopped
2 tsp. sugar
1 tsp. Italian seasoning
1 tsp. salt
10 oz. frozen peas, thawed
1 12 1/2-oz. can tuna, drained
2 medium firm tomatoes, chopped

Prepare linguine according to package directions; drain. Meanwhile, in a large bowl mix lemon juice, oil, onions, sugar, Italian seasoning, and salt. Add hot pasta and toss. Stir in remaining ingredients and mix well. Cover and chill for 2 hours or overnight.

Seafood Pasta Salad

2 c. tri-colored spiral pasta
1 c. cooked shrimp
1/3 c. green pepper, diced
1/4 c. carrots, sliced
1/2 c. zucchini, sliced
1/3 c. white wine Worcestershire sauce
1/3 c. mayonnaise
salt and pepper to taste

Prepare pasta according to package directions. Rinse and drain well. In a mixing bowl, combine pasta, shrimp, bell pepper, carrots and zucchini. Mix in Worcestershire, mayonnaise, salt, and pepper. Refrigerate at least 2 hours before serving.

Garlic Shrimp and Pasta

2 tbsp. cornstarch
1 14 1/2-oz. can chicken broth
2 cloves garlic, minced
1 tbsp. dried parsley flakes
2 tbsp. lemon juice
1/8 tsp. ground red pepper
1 lb. medium shrimp, shelled and deveined
4 c. thin spaghetti, cooked and hot

In medium saucepan mix cornstarch, broth, garlic, parsley, lemon juice and pepper. Cook over medium-high heat until mixture boils and thickens, stirring constantly. Add shrimp and cook for 5 minutes or until shrimp turn pink, stirring often. Toss with spaghetti.

Shrimp with Tomato Cream Pasta

1/3 c. dried tomatoes packed in oil, drained
   and cut into slivers (reserve 2 tbsp. oil)
1 clove garlic, minced
1 lb. large shrimp, shelled and deveined
1/4 c. green onion, thinly sliced
1 tsp. dried basil
1/4 tsp. ground white pepper
1 c. chicken broth
3/4 c. dry vermouth
1 c. whipping cream
10 oz. dry linguini
Parmesan cheese, freshly grated

Heat 2 tablespoons oil from dried tomatoes and garlic in a large frying pan over medium-high heat. When hot, add shrimp and cook, stirring often, until opaque in center, about 6 minutes. Use slotted spoon and remove shrimp; set aside.

To the pan, add onion, basil, dried tomatoes, pepper, broth, vermouth, and cream. Boil on high heat, uncovered, until reduced to about 1 1/2 cups, about 10 minutes.

Add shrimp and stir until hot. Meanwhile, cook pasta in 3 quarts boiling water until just tender to bite, about 8 minutes; drain well.

Add cooked pasta to sauce and lift with 2 forks to blend. Serve with Parmesan cheese.

Shrimp and Chicken Spaghetti

1 7-oz. pkg. spaghetti
1/2 lb. skinless and boneless chicken
   breast, cubed
1 medium onion, diced
3 cloves garlic, minced
1 small green pepper, diced
1 small sweet red pepper, cut into strips
1 28-oz. can whole plum tomatoes, crushed
1/4 tsp. red pepper flakes
1/2 tsp. salt
oregano, marjoram, and basil to taste
1/2 lb. raw shrimp, shelled and deveined

Prepare pasta according to package directions; drain. Meanwhile, sauté chicken, vegetables and spices until chicken is firm and onions are translucent. Simmer, uncovered, over low heat for 1/2 hour. Turn off heat and add shrimp. (Residual heat will cook shrimp.) Wait 10 minutes and serve over spaghetti.

Lemon Scallop Spaghetti

4 tbsp. margarine
16 oz. fresh scallops
2 14-oz. cans chicken broth
1 c. water
1 c. lemon juice, freshly squeezed
2 tbsp. honey
2 tsp. lemon peel, finely grated
1 1/2 tsp. dried rosemary
salt and pepper to taste
16 oz. spaghetti

Melt margarine in a large saucepan over medium heat. Add scallops and sauté until cooked through, about 4-5 minutes.

Add all remaining ingredients except spaghetti to pan. Bring mixture to a boil and add spaghetti.

Reduce heat, cover and simmer for about 15 minutes, stirring occasionally. Serve immediately.

Salmon and Spinach Noodle Bake

12 oz. medium or wide egg noodles
2 tbsp. vegetable or olive oil
2 leeks, chopped
2 cloves garlic, minced
1/3 c. flour
2 c. milk
2 tbsp. Dijon mustard
2 tbsp. fresh dill, chopped *or* 1 tsp. dried dill
salt and fresh ground black pepper to taste
2 pkg. (10 oz. ea.) frozen chopped spinach,
   thawed and squeezed dry
2 cans (14.75 oz. ea.) red salmon,
   or 1 lb. fresh salmon, poached and skin and
   bones removed
vegetable oil cooking spray
garnish (optional): 2 oz. smoked salmon,
   cut into thin strips; fresh spinach leaves;
   fresh dill sprigs; roasted red peppers;
   lemon slices

Preheat oven to 350°F. Cook noodles until *al dente*. Drain and set aside.

While noodles are cooking, heat oil over medium-high heat in large saucepan. Add leeks and garlic and sauté, stirring occasionally, until leeks are softened, about 5 minutes.

Add flour and cook, stirring constantly, 2 more minutes. Gradually add milk, stirring constantly.

Bring to a boil; reduce heat and simmer, stirring constantly, until thickened, about 10 minutes. Stir in mustard, dill, and salt and pepper to taste.

Add spinach, salmon, and cooked noodles to cream mixture; blend well.

Spray a 10-inch ring mold with cooking spray. Transfer noodle mixture into mold and press lightly. Bake 20-25 minutes.

Loosen edges with a knife and invert onto platter. Garnish as desired.

Fettuccine With Vegetables and Scallops

12 oz. fettuccine
2 tbsp. olive or vegetable oil
2 stalks celery, julienned
1 red bell pepper, julienned
2 carrots, julienned
3 green onions, julienned
1 lb. raw ocean scallops or bay scallops
1/2 c. fresh orange juice
red pepper flakes to taste
1 tsp. orange zest, grated
3/4 c. Romano cheese, grated
parsley for garnish

Cook pasta according to package directions; drain. Heat oil in large skillet; add celery, pepper, carrots, and green onions.

Cook, tossing until tender-crisp. Slice scallops in thirds (bay scallops can be used whole). Add to vegetables and toss until opaque, about 1-2 minutes.

Add orange juice, pepper flakes, and orange zest. Cook 2 more minutes; pour over cooked pasta. Toss with cheese and garnish with parsley.

Rotini With Tuna and Tomato

8 oz. Rotini, twists, or spirals
1 can (6 1/8 oz.) solid white tuna packed
  in water, drained
1 medium zucchini, diced
1 green bell pepper, ribs and seeds removed, diced
1 medium tomato, peeled, seeded, and chopped
3 scallions, sliced
1/4 c. capers, drained (optional)
2 tbsp. vegetable or olive oil
2 tbsp. lemon juice
1 tsp. fresh basil, minced
2 tbsp. fresh parsley, minced
fresh ground pepper to taste

Cook pasta according to package directions; drain and chill. Combine pasta, tuna, zucchini, bell pepper, tomato, scallions, and capers; toss. Mix remaining ingredients and pour over pasta mixture. Toss lightly and serve.

Mostaccioli and Shrimp With Tangerine-Basil Sauce

5 1/2 c. tangerine or orange juice, divided
1 large yellow onion, minced
1 tbsp. jalapeño pepper, minced and seeded
2 bay leaves
2 tbsp. minced garlic, divided
salt and fresh ground pepper to taste
1 lb. mostaccioli
1 tbsp. olive or vegetable oil
1 medium red onion, sliced thin
1 lb. medium shrimp, peeled and deveined
1 c. (4 oz.) Brie cheese, diced
2 tbsp. basil leaves, sliced thin
1 c. tangerine or orange segments
1/3 c. almonds, slivered and lightly toasted

Combine 5 cups tangerine or orange juice, yellow onion, jalapeño, bay leaves, and 1 tablespoon of garlic in a medium saucepan. Bring to a boil and cook until liquid is reduced by two-thirds.

Remove bay leaves. Allow to cool. Transfer juice mixture to a blender and blend until smooth. Add salt and pepper to taste and set aside.

Prepare pasta according to package directions. While pasta is cooking, add oil, red onion, and shrimp to a medium skillet. Sauté 1 minute. Add remaining tangerine or orange juice to skillet and cook over low heat.

Drain pasta, return it to pot and add orange sauce and shrimp mixture. Cook over low heat 1 minute. Add Brie and basil and stir until Brie is melted. Transfer to a serving bowl. Garnish with tangerine or orange segments and toasted almonds. Serve immediately.

Shrimp and Crab Spaghetti

2 medium onions, chopped
1 clove garlic, minced
2 tbsp. vegetable oil
1 c. tomato paste
1 tsp. basil
1/2 tsp. salt
1 stick butter
2 cans (8 oz. ea.) tomato sauce
1 tbsp. chili powder
1/2 tsp. sugar
1/4 tsp. pepper
2 lb. peeled shrimp
12 crabs, cooked or raw
1 pkg. spaghetti, cooked

Brown onions and garlic in hot oil. Add all remaining ingredients except shrimp, crabs, and spaghetti. Bring to boil and simmer 30 minutes, stirring constantly. Remove outer shell and legs from crabs, leaving meat in bottom part; break in half. Add shrimp and crabs to sauce; simmer for an additional 30 minutes or until crabs are done. Pour sauce over cooked spaghetti.

Angel Hair Pasta With Shrimp

1 1/2 tbsp. butter
1 1/2 tbsp. flour
1 1/2 c. milk
1/2 c. cream
1 1/2 tbsp. pesto sauce
1 1/2 tbsp. parsley, chopped
1 tbsp. garlic, minced
2 tbsp. Parmesan cheese, grated
1/2 tsp. salt
1/2 tsp. white pepper
dash Worcestershire sauce
dash hot red pepper sauce
2/3 lb. capellini
1/2 red pepper, cut into strips
1/4 lb. snow peas, trimmed
1 lb. jumbo shrimp

In a saucepan over medium heat, melt butter, stir in flour and cook for a few minutes until golden. Add milk and cream; bring to a gentle simmer and continue to stir until thickened.

Add pesto, parsley, garlic, Parmesan, salt, pepper, Worcestershire sauce, and pepper sauce; stir until blended. Reduce heat and keep warm, stirring occasionally. Cook pasta quickly in a large pot of boiling water (3-4 minutes or until *al dente*).

Meanwhile, poach white pepper, snowpeas, and shrimp in another pot of boiling water for 2-3 minutes or until just heated through. Drain pasta.

Mix pasta and sauce and portion into heated individual serving bowls. Garnish each portion with shrimp and vegetables; serve immediately.

Shellfish Shell Marinara

3 tsp. extra-virgin olive oil
2 large garlic slices, peeled and bruised
2 cans (28 oz.) plum tomatoes, drained
  and chopped coarse
1/4 c. dry red wine
1/4 c. coarsely chopped parsley
1/4 c. fresh basil leaves, torn in half
1 tsp. dried oregano
salt and fresh ground black pepper to taste
pinch sugar
12 oz. medium-sized pasta shells
20 littleneck clams
1/2 lb. large shrimp, peeled and deveined

Place oil in a large, heavy pot over medium-low heat. Add garlic and cook for 3-4 minutes, until it colors slightly but does not burn. Remove garlic from heat and carefully stir in tomatoes.

Return pot to medium heat. Add wine, parsley, basil, oregano, salt, pepper, and sugar. Cook sauce slowly, stirring occasionally, for 30 minutes.

Slightly before serving, cook pasta in boiling, salted water for 10-12 minutes or until *al dente*.

While pasta is cooking, add clams to sauce; cover and cook for 8 minutes or until clams just begin to open, shaking pot once or twice. Add shrimp and cook 5 minutes longer. (Discard any clams that don't open, as they could be unsafe to eat.)

Divide cooked pasta among six shallow bowls. Spoon hot sauce over top, distributing clams and shrimp evenly. Serve immediately.

Pasta with Chicken

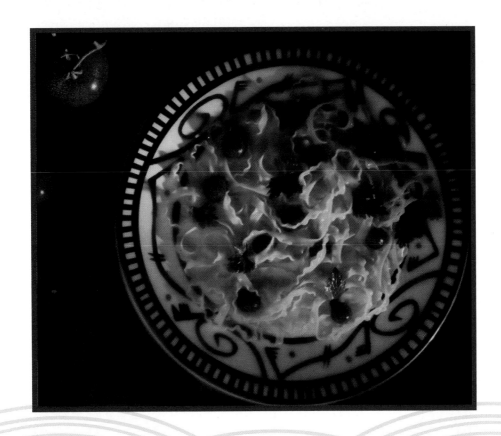

Cube:
To cut into uniform-sized pieces that are about
1/2-inch on each side.

Dice:
To cut into uniform-sized pieces
1/8- to 1/4-inch on each side.

Garlic Pasta Chicken Salad

8 oz. Rotini
6 cloves fresh garlic
3/4 c. olive oil
1/4 c. fresh basil leaves
1 tsp. dried rosemary
2 c. chicken, cooked and cut into strips
1/2 c. green onion, sliced
1/2 c. Parmesan cheese, freshly grated
salt and pepper to taste
1/2 c. walnuts, chopped
lettuce

Prepare pasta according to package directions; drain. Separate cloves of garlic and drop into boiling water for 1 minute. Drain and peel. Place peeled cloves in small saucepan with oil. Cover and cook gently, stirring occasionally, for about 25 minutes or until garlic is tender. Purée garlic with 1/2 cup olive oil, basil, and rosemary.

Place pasta in large bowl and add garlic purée, chicken, onion, Parmesan cheese, salt, and pepper. Mix thoroughly. Let salad sit for 1 hour at room temperature or refrigerate, returning mixture to room temperature before serving. Toast walnuts in 375°F oven for 10 minutes. Stir into salad and serve over a mix of crisp, chilled lettuce.

Citrus Chicken Pasta

1 lb. elbow macaroni
12 oz. chicken, cooked and cut into
   1/2-inch pieces
3 c. seedless red grapes
1 20-oz. can unsweetened pineapple
   chunks, drained
1/2 c. mayonnaise
2 tbsp. lemon juice
1/4 c. frozen orange juice concentrate, thawed
1 tbsp. curry powder

Prepare pasta according to package directions; drain. Meanwhile, toss chicken, grapes and pineapple together in a large bowl. In a medium bowl stir together mayonnaise, lemon juice, orange juice concentrate and curry powder. Toss together fruit mixture and pasta. Add mayonnaise mixture and mix well.

Chicken Spaghetti

4 skinless and boneless chicken breasts
12 oz. spaghetti
1 onion, finely chopped
1 tbsp. butter
1/2 lb. processed cheese, cubed
1 small can tomatoes, diced
1 small can green chilies
1 large can cream of chicken soup

Boil chicken breasts until cooked. Cut into bite size pieces. Cook spaghetti in chicken broth. In large pan, sauté the onion in butter until soft. Add chicken, cheese, tomatoes, chilies, and soup. Simmer until all cheese is melted, stirring often. Add spaghetti and mix well.

Easy Chicken Fettuccine

8 oz. fettuccine
2 skinless and boneless chicken breast
   halves, cubed
1/2 c. milk
1/4 c. margarine, softened
3/4 c. Parmesan cheese
3/4 tsp. garlic powder
salt and pepper to taste

Prepare fettuccine according to package directions; drain. Meanwhile, cook chicken in skillet sprayed with cooking spray until cooked through. Toss fettuccine with milk and margarine. Stir in chicken and remaining ingredients.

Spaghetti with Chicken Sauce

1/4 c. olive oil
1 onion, diced
2 cloves garlic, finely chopped
2 large cans tomato purée
1 large can tomato paste
salt and pepper to taste
sugar to taste
2 chicken breasts, fried and cubed
1/2 tsp. basil
1 tsp. oregano
1 pkg. spaghetti, cooked

In large sauce pan, heat olive oil on medium-high until hot. Add onion and sauté 8 minutes; add garlic and continue to sauté until onion is golden brown. Drain and discard oil.

Reduce temperature to medium. Add purée to pan and stir. Empty paste into a bowl, then fill empty paste can with water. Stir to remove remaining paste; add this to bowl. Whisk slowly until mixed. Add to purée. Fill the empty purée can with water, stir to remove all remaining purée, and add this to pan. Add salt, pepper, and sugar to taste. Add onion and chicken and stir.

Cook, covered, over medium heat for an hour or until sauce is as thick as you like, stirring often. Add any herbs during the last 5-10 minutes of cooking. Serve over cooked spaghetti.

Quick Chicken Parmesan

4 skinless and boneless chicken breast halves
2 c. prepared spaghetti sauce
1/2 c. mozzarella cheese, shredded
2 tbsp. Parmesan cheese, grated
4 c. spaghetti, cooked and hot

Preheat oven to 400°F. Place chicken in 2-quart shallow baking dish. Pour spaghetti sauce over chicken; top with mozzarella and Parmesan cheeses. Bake for 25 minutes or until chicken is no longer pink. Serve with spaghetti.

Baked Chicken and Pasta Casserole

12 oz. medium egg noodles, uncooked
1 tbsp. vegetable oil
8 oz. boneless and skinless chicken breast meat, cubed
1 small red onion, diced
3 tsp. curry powder
1 1/2 c. chicken broth
1 1/2 tbsp. cornstarch
1 10-oz. can evaporated skim milk
1 c. frozen peas
1 1/2 c. fresh mushrooms, sliced
1 tbsp. lemon juice
salt and pepper to taste
2 tbsp. dry bread crumbs

Prepare pasta according to package directions; drain. Meanwhile, preheat oven to 375°F. Heat oil in a large heavy skillet over medium-high heat. Add chicken and onion and stir until chicken begins to brown, about 4 minutes. Add curry powder and continue stirring 2 minutes. Add chicken broth and reduce heat to low.

In a small bowl, dissolve cornstarch in evaporated skim milk. Stir cornstarch mixture into skillet and heat to simmering. Continue to simmer 2 minutes, then pour contents of skillet into a large bowl.

Stir in cooked pasta, peas, mushrooms, lemon juice, salt, and pepper to curry sauce. Pour mixture into an 11x9-inch baking dish and sprinkle bread crumbs on top. Bake until edges are bubbling and crumbs are golden brown, about 15 minutes.

19

Chicken Lasagne

1 lb. skinless and boneless chicken
   breast meat, diced
4 c. spaghetti sauce
1 1/2 c. water
2 tbsp. hot sauce
2 tbsp. vinegar
1 tsp. garlic salt
15 oz. ricotta cheese
1 egg, beaten
12 pieces lasagna, uncooked
3/4 c. blue cheese, crumbled

Preheat oven to 350°F. Sauté chicken 4 minutes over medium-high heat in a large skillet sprayed with cooking spray. Drain well. Stir in spaghetti sauce, water, hot sauce, vinegar, and garlic salt.

In a small bowl, combine ricotta cheese and egg; set aside. Spray a 9x13-inch baking pan with cooking spray. Spread 1 cup of sauce over bottom of pan. Arrange 4 pieces of lasagna over sauce. Cover with 1 1/2 cups of sauce. Spread half ricotta mixture on top. Arrange another 4 pieces of lasagna over ricotta, and top with another 1 1/2 cups of sauce. Spread remaining ricotta mixture on top. Arrange final 4 pieces of lasagna over ricotta mixture and cover with remaining sauce.

Cover lasagna with foil and bake for 1 hour and 10 minutes. Remove from oven and uncover. Sprinkle blue cheese on top and bake, uncovered, an additional 5 minutes. Cover and let stand 15 minutes before serving.

Chicken and Broccoli Pasta Dijon

1 lb. penne pasta, uncooked
8 oz. boneless and skinless chicken breast
   meat, cubed
1/2 tsp. salt
1/4 tsp. black pepper, freshly ground
2 cloves garlic, minced
2 tsp. vegetable oil
3 c. broccoli florets
1 large red bell pepper, chopped
1/2 c. chicken broth
1 12-oz. can evaporated skim milk
1 tbsp. cornstarch
3 tbsp. Dijon mustard

Prepare pasta according to package directions; drain well. Meanwhile, toss chicken with salt, pepper and garlic. Coat a large non-stick skillet or wok with cooking spray; heat over medium-high heat until hot. Add oil to skillet; stir-fry chicken mixture in oil, 4 to 5 minutes or until chicken is cooked through.

Remove chicken from skillet and place in a medium bowl. Add broccoli, red pepper and chicken broth to skillet. Cover and simmer over medium heat, 5 to 6 minutes or until vegetables are tender-crisp. Transfer to bowl with chicken.

In a small bowl, combine 1/4 cup of milk with cornstarch, mixing until cornstarch is dissolved. Add cornstarch mixture to skillet with remaining milk and bring to a boil, stirring constantly. Reduce heat. Stir in mustard and reserved chicken mixture. Toss pasta with chicken mixture. Serve immediately.

Chicken Noodle Casserole

8 oz. egg noodles
1/2 c. sour cream
1 c. chicken broth
4 tbsp. Parmesan cheese, grated and divided
1 egg, beaten
2 tbsp. Dijon mustard
1 1/2 c. broccoli, chopped and drained
1 1/2 c. skinless and boneless chicken
　breast meat, cooked
2 tbsp. bread crumbs

Prepare egg noodles according to package directions; drain. Preheat oven to 350°F. Stir together sour cream, chicken broth, 2 tablespoons Parmesan cheese, egg, and mustard in a bowl until blended. Add noodles, broccoli, and chicken; toss well.

Transfer mixture to a 9x12-inch baking dish. Mix remaining 2 tablespoons of grated cheese with bread crumbs and sprinkle over casserole. Bake, uncovered, until bubbling around edges and top is golden brown, about 35 minutes. Let stand 5 minutes before serving.

Chicken Mushroom Fettuccine

12 oz. fettuccine
8 oz. boneless and skinless chicken breast
　meat, cubed
8 oz. mushrooms, sliced
1/2 c. red bell pepper, diced
1 1/2 c. mayonnaise
3/4 c. milk
1/4 c. Parmesan cheese
1 tsp. dried basil
1 tsp. pepper
1/2 tsp. paprika

Prepare pasta according to package directions; drain and return to pot. Meanwhile, spray large skillet with cooking spray. Sauté chicken over medium-high heat, stirring frequently, until chicken is golden brown and cooked through, about 4 minutes. Remove chicken from pan.

Recoat skillet with cooking spray. Sauté mushrooms and red pepper until tender, about 5 minutes. In a small bowl, combine mayonnaise, milk, Parmesan cheese, basil, pepper, and paprika. Add to vegetables in skillet. Add chicken to skillet; continue to cook over medium-low heat, stirring constantly, until thoroughly heated. Add contents of skillet to pot of pasta and mix well. Serve immediately.

Quick Chicken Casserole

8 oz. ziti
2 tbsp. margarine, divided
8 oz. mushrooms, sliced
3 tbsp. all-purpose flour
1 tbsp. Dijon mustard
1 3/4 c. milk
1/2 tsp. salt
2 (5-oz.) cans chunk white chicken, drained
　and flaked
1/3 c. Parmesan cheese, grated
salt and pepper to taste

Preheat oven to 350°F. Prepare pasta according to package directions; drain. Return pasta to pot. Meanwhile, melt 1 tablespoon margarine in a skillet over medium-high heat. Sauté mushrooms 2 to 3 minutes. Drain off any liquid and set mushrooms aside.

Place remaining margarine in skillet and melt over medium-low heat. Stir in flour with a wire whisk. Gradually add Dijon mustard, milk, and salt. Stir constantly until mixture boils and thickens. Once thickened, stir in mushrooms and remove from heat. Add chicken, mushroom mixture, cheese, salt, and pepper to pasta. Transfer all ingredients to a 2-quart casserole dish. Bake for 15 minutes or until heated through. Serve immediately.

Chicken and Red Pesto Linguine

1 lb. uncooked linguine, broken in half

1 jar (8-oz.) sun-dried tomatoes packed
   in olive oil, drained

4 tbsp. olive oil or vegetable oil, divided

4 tbsp. fresh oregano, chopped or 4 tsp.
   dried oregano

3 cloves garlic

1-2 tsp. fresh grated lemon peel or 1 tsp.
   bottled lemon juice

1/3 c. fresh Parmesan cheese, grated

1 lb. boneless skinless chicken breasts,
   cut into 1-inch pieces

1 c. sliced scallions, white and green parts

1 can (14-oz.) artichoke hearts, drained
   and chopped

Prepare pasta according to package directions.
While pasta is cooking, combine drained sun-dried
tomatoes, 1 tablespoon oil, oregano, garlic, and
lemon peel or juice in food processor or blender.
Process until smooth, scraping side of container.
Add cheese; process until well blended.

Heat chicken in remaining oil in large skillet for 3
minutes over medium heat, stirring frequently. Stir
in scallions. Cook 3 minutes longer. Add artichokes
and heat 1 minute.

Drain pasta. Place in large bowl. Add sun-dried
tomato pesto and chicken mixture and toss. Serve
immediately garnished with fresh grated Parmesan
cheese, if desired.

Bow Ties With Asian Chicken

4 tbsp. soy sauce

2 tbsp. honey

2 tbsp. lime juice

3 tsp. Dijon mustard with seeds

1 lb. boneless, skinless chicken breasts,
   cut into 1/2-inch cubes

1/2 c. chicken broth or pasta cooking liquid

1 lb. bow ties, uncooked

2 small red bell peppers, cored, seeded
   and sliced thin lengthwise

6 scallions, trimmed and sliced thin

pepper, freshly ground

4 tbsp. fresh parsley, chopped

Stir soy sauce, honey, lime juice, and mustard
in a small bowl until honey is dissolved. Add
chicken pieces and turn until coated with
marinade. Refrigerate for 30 minutes.

Transfer chicken and marinade to a large, non-
stick skillet. Cook over medium heat until
chicken is cooked through, about 4 minutes.
Remove from heat and pour in chicken broth.

Prepare pasta according to package directions.
Drain thoroughly in a colander. Return pasta to
pot. Add skillet contents, red peppers, and
scallions.

Heat to simmering over low heat. Toss pasta
once or twice. Add pepper to taste and divide
among serving bowls. Sprinkle each serving
with chopped fresh parsley.

Pasta with Vegetables

Mince:
To cut a food into very tiny, irregular-shaped pieces.

Ricotta:
A soft, Italian cottage cheese made with skim milk.

Pasta with Spicy Cucumber Sauce

2 cucumbers, peeled, seeded, and coarsely grated
2 tbsp. yellow onion, minced
2 c. plain yogurt
1 clove garlic, minced
2 green onions, chopped
1 small tomato, finely chopped
2 tbsp. lemon juice
2 tbsp. fresh parsley, finely minced
2 tsp. ground cumin
black pepper, freshly ground
salt
1 lb. pasta

Combine grated cucumber and onion in a small, non-metallic bowl. Sprinkle with salt and let stand for 10 minutes. Drain and squeeze dry. Whisk yogurt until creamy smooth. Add cucumber mixture, garlic, green onions, tomato, lemon juice, minced parsley, and cumin. Add salt and pepper to taste and mix thoroughly. Chill overnight.

Cook pasta in 4 quarts boiling water until very *al dente*. Drain and rinse well in cold water, then drain again. Place in a large bowl and cool to room temperature, stirring occasionally to keep pasta from sticking together. Combine pasta with yogurt mixture and serve.

Tomato and Basil Pasta

8 oz. pasta
3 c. ripe tomatoes, chopped
1/2 c. fresh basil
2 tbsp. olive oil
1 clove garlic, minced
1/4 tsp. salt
1/4 tsp. ground black pepper
1/2 c. feta cheese, crumbled

Cook pasta according to package directions; drain. Mix tomatoes, basil, oil, garlic, salt, and pepper. Toss mixture with pasta and feta cheese. Serve immediately.

Spinach and Bacon Bowtie Pasta

12 oz. bowtie pasta, uncooked
2 tbsp. olive oil
2 cloves garlic, chopped
10 oz. frozen spinach, chopped and thawed
1/2 c. dry white wine
1/2 c. Parmesan cheese, grated
1 12-oz. pkg. bacon, crisply cooked
  and crumbled
pepper to taste

Prepare pasta according to package directions. Drain pasta and reserve 1/2 cup of cooking water. Heat oil in large skillet over medium heat. Sauté garlic in hot oil for 1 minute. Increase heat to medium-high. Stir in spinach, wine, and reserved 1/2 cup cooking water. Cook and stir until thoroughly heated. Add pasta and cheese to spinach mixture. Sprinkle all with bacon. Season to taste with pepper.

Quick-Baked Creamy Pasta

1 jar spaghetti sauce
1 16-oz. package Rotini, cooked and drained
1 1/2 c. sour cream
1 10-oz. pkg. frozen spinach, chopped,
  thawed and drained
1/2 c. Parmesan cheese, grated

Preheat oven to 375°F. Mix all ingredients. Spoon into 13x9-inch baking dish. Bake for 25 minutes.

Mostaccioli with Spinach

8 oz. mostaccioli
2 tbsp. olive oil
3 c. tomatoes, chopped
4 c. fresh spinach, washed and stems removed
1/2 c. green onions, chopped
1 8-oz. pkg. feta cheese
1/2 tbsp. basil

Cook pasta according to package directions. Drain and return to pot. Stir in oil, tomatoes, spinach and onions. Cook 2 minutes or until spinach is wilted and mixture is thoroughly heated, stirring constantly. Add feta cheese and basil and cook 1 minute.

Spinach Lasagne

16 oz. cottage cheese
10 oz. frozen spinach, thawed, chopped
   and drained
3 c. mozzarella cheese, shredded and divided
1 c. Parmesan cheese, grated and divided
2 eggs, beaten
1 jar spaghetti sauce, divided
9 lasagna noodles, cooked, drained

Preheat oven to 350°F. Mix cottage cheese, spinach, 2 cups mozzarella cheese, 1/2 cup Parmesan cheese, and eggs.

Layer 1 cup of spaghetti sauce, 3 lasagna noodles and 1/2 cottage cheese mixture in 13x9-inch baking dish. Repeat layer once and then top with remaining 3 noodles, 1 cup sauce, 1 cup mozzarella cheese and 1/2 cup Parmesan cheese.

Bake 45 minutes. Let stand 10 minutes before serving.

Country Fettuccine

1 carrot, peeled and cut into thin strips
24 asparagus spears, trimmed and cut
   into 2-inch pieces
12 oz. fettuccine
2 tsp. vegetable oil
1 c. leeks, thinly sliced
1 small yellow bell pepper, cut into thin strips
2 c. whipping cream
1/2 c. Parmesan cheese, grated
2/3 c. country ham, diced
salt and pepper to taste

Bring large pot of salted water to boil. Add carrot and cook 4 minutes. Use slotted spoon to transfer carrot to strainer; cool. Add asparagus to boiling water and cook until just tender, about 3 minutes. Using slotted spoon, remove asparagus pieces, reserving tips for garnish.

Add pasta to boiling water and cook until just tender but still *al dente*, stirring occasionally. Drain pasta and return to pot.

Meanwhile, heat oil in large, heavy skillet over medium-high heat. Sauté leeks and bell pepper for 2 minutes. Add cream and simmer until slightly thickened, about 5 minutes. Mix in grated Parmesan cheese and country ham. Add carrot and asparagus pieces to sauce. Season to taste with salt and pepper.

Pour sauce over pasta and toss to coat evenly. Serve, using asparagus tips for garnish and adding additional Parmesan cheese to taste.

Fettuccine with Spinach Sauce

16 oz. fettuccine noodles
1 medium onion, chopped
3 cloves garlic, minced
3 tbsp. olive oil
1 1/4 c. ricotta cheese
1 c. milk
2/3 c. Parmesan cheese, grated
1 10-oz. pkg. frozen spinach, thawed, drained and chopped
3 tomatoes, chopped
salt and pepper to taste

Prepare pasta according to package directions. Meanwhile, sauté onion and garlic in oil until tender. Add ricotta cheese, milk, and Parmesan cheese. Cook mixture for 2 minutes and add spinach. Cook on medium-low heat until thoroughly heated. Stir in tomatoes. Toss sauce with hot cooked fettuccine. Season to taste with salt and pepper.

Fresh Tomato and Basil Pasta

8 oz. Rotini
3 medium tomatoes, chopped
1 tsp. dried basil
1/4 c. olive oil
1 clove garlic, minced
1/2 tsp. salt
1/2 tsp. pepper
3/4 c. Parmesan cheese, grated

Prepare Rotini according to package directions. Meanwhile, combine tomatoes, basil, oil, garlic, salt and pepper. Toss drained Rotini with tomato mixture and cheese. Serve immediately.

Eggplant Parmesan

1 eggplant
1/2 c. whole wheat flour
1 tsp. salt, divided
3 egg whites
1/4 c. milk
2 c. bread crumbs
1 tsp. oregano
1/2 tsp. cayenne pepper
1/4 tsp. pepper
2 c. tomato sauce
1/2 c. Parmesan cheese, grated
1 c. mozzarella cheese

Preheat oven to 350°F. Slice eggplant into 1/4-inch thick rounds. In one bowl combine flour and 1/2 teaspoon salt. In another bowl mix egg whites and milk. Use a third bowl to mix bread crumbs and remaining 1/2 teaspoon salt, oregano, and peppers.

Cover eggplant slices in flour, then egg and milk mixture, and then bread crumb mixture. Make a layer of coated slices in a casserole dish and sprinkle with 1 cup tomato sauce and 1/4 cup Parmesan cheese. Make another layer of slices on the first layer, staggering slices so they do not completely overlap lower slices. Sprinkle second layer with remaining 1 cup tomato sauce and 1/4 cup Parmesan cheese.

Cover casserole and bake for 45 minutes. Remove casserole and sprinkle with mozzarella cheese; return to oven for 5 minutes until cheese is melted.

Eggplant Lasagne

1 1/4 lb. eggplant
1/2 c. olive oil
1 tsp. dried basil
3 cloves garlic, minced
1 tsp. dried oregano
8 oz. mozzarella cheese
15 oz. ricotta cheese
2 c. spaghetti sauce
2 tsp. fennel seed
1/2 c. ripe olives, sliced

Preheat oven to 425°F. Cut eggplant into thin slices. Mix olive oil with herbs and brush both sides of eggplant slices. In a non-stick skillet, brown eggplant slices on both sides until tender. Make layers starting with half eggplant slices, mozzarella, ricotta, spaghetti sauce, fennel seed and olives in an oiled, oven-safe casserole dish. Repeat the layers. Top with remaining mozzarella and cover. Bake for 25 minutes until hot and bubbly. Let stand 15 minutes before serving.

Lemon Pasta with Roasted Asparagus

10 asparagus stalks, ends snapped
1 tbsp. olive oil, divided
1/2 tsp. salt, divided
12 oz. fettuccine
1 c. dry white wine
3 shallots, chopped
3 lemons
1 1/2 c. whipping cream
1/3 c. plus 2 tbsp. Parmesan cheese, grated and divided
1/8 tsp. cayenne pepper
4 tbsp. butter
1 tbsp. minced chives

Preheat oven to 425°F. Wash and dry asparagus. Place stalks in a baking pan large enough to hold them in one layer, and gently rub them with 1/2 tablespoon olive oil.

Sprinkle 1/4 teaspoon salt over asparagus and bake for 12 minutes. When cool enough to handle, cut into 1/2-inch pieces.

In a generous amount of salted boiling water, cook fettuccine until *al dente*; drain. Place fettuccine in a bowl and toss with 1/2 tablespoon olive oil.

Pour wine into a large skillet or pan and add shallots. Reduce liquid, over medium heat, to one half.

Wash lemons well. Add grated rind and juice from 2 lemons to wine. Simmer 2 minutes. Add cream and bring mixture to a boil.

Lower heat and add 1/3 cup cheese, 1/4 teaspoon salt, and cayenne pepper. Simmer slowly, stirring constantly, until sauce begins to thicken.

Cut cold butter into small pieces and add to sauce, cooking 1 minute. Add asparagus, pasta and 2 tablespoons cheese. Toss until pasta is thoroughly coated with sauce and heated through.

Divide pasta evenly; sprinkle with chives and grated peel from remaining lemon.

Vegetable Lasagne

3 cloves garlic, minced
1/2 white onion, finely chopped
2 tbsp. olive oil, divided
2 15-oz. cans tomato purée
1 tbsp. dried basil
2 tbsp. oregano
1 tbsp. dried parsley
salt and pepper to taste
1/2 red bell pepper
2 carrots
1 small head broccoli
1 medium zucchini
3-4 large mushrooms
8 oz. ricotta cheese
12 oz. mozzarella cheese, shredded
1 lb. lasagna noodles

Preheat oven to 375°F. Sauté garlic and onion in 1 tablespoon olive oil. Pour in tomato purée. Add herbs, salt, and pepper to taste; simmer.

Meanwhile, chop vegetables and sauté in remaining tablespoon of olive oil. Drop pasta in boiling water and simmer for 8-10 minutes. Rinse well and drain thoroughly.

Spread a thin layer of sauce in a 9x12-inch baking dish. Layer 1/3 noodles, 1/2 vegetables, ricotta, and a bit less than 1/2 mozzarella and sauce. Repeat for second layer. Top with remaining noodles, sauce, and cheese.

Cover tightly with foil and bake for 30 minutes. Uncover and sprinkle with Parmesan cheese. Bake for 10 more minutes. Let stand for 10 minutes before slicing.

Fast Primavera

1 lb. mostaccioli
1 head broccoli, cut into small florets
1 tbsp. cornstarch
1/4 c. water
3 cloves garlic, minced
1 15 1/2-oz. can chicken broth
1 10-oz. pkg. frozen mixed vegetables
1 10-oz. pkg. frozen spinach, chopped
   and thawed
salt and pepper to taste
1 c. Parmesan cheese, grated

Prepare pasta according to package directions. Three minutes before pasta is done, stir in broccoli. Drain pasta and vegetables and place in a large serving bowl.

In another bowl, dissolve cornstarch in water. In a large saucepan, simmer garlic with chicken broth over medium heat for 3 minutes.

Whisk in cornstarch. Stir in mixed vegetables and spinach and cook until hot, about 5 minutes. Toss sauce and vegetables with pasta.

Season with salt and pepper, sprinkle with Parmesan cheese, and serve.

Three Bean Pasta

1 lb. medium or wide egg noodles
1 can (15 oz.) kidney beans, rinsed and drained
1 can (15 oz.) chickpeas, rinsed and drained
1 c. frozen green beans, thawed
1 small red onion, chopped
1 red bell pepper, seeds and ribs removed, chopped
3 tbsp. Dijon mustard
2 tbsp. vegetable oil
3 tbsp. red wine vinegar
3 tbsp. fresh parsley, chopped

Prepare pasta according to package directions; drain. Rinse under cold water and drain again.

In a large bowl, stir together pasta, kidney beans, chickpeas, green beans, onion, and bell pepper. In a small bowl, stir together remaining ingredients. Toss pasta with dressing and serve.

Primavera With Zucchini, Tomato, and Corn

1 lb. mostaccioli, medium shells, or
   other medium pasta shape
1 tbsp. vegetable oil
1 clove garlic, minced
1 medium red onion, chopped
2 c. zucchini, chopped
2 c. fresh tomato, chopped
1 c. fresh corn or 1 c. frozen corn, thawed
1/2 tsp. hot red pepper flakes
1 c. skim milk
1/2 c. Parmesan cheese, freshly grated
1/4 c. Italian flat-leaf parsley, minced
salt and fresh ground pepper to taste

Prepare pasta according to package directions; drain. Heat oil in a large skillet. Add garlic, red onion, and zucchini; cook over medium-high heat until garlic and onion are golden.

Reduce heat to medium and add tomato, corn, red pepper flakes, skim milk, and Parmesan cheese. Stir until cheese is melted and vegetables are hot. Add pasta and parsley. Mix thoroughly. Season with salt and pepper to taste.

Acorn Squash 'n Pasta Soup

8 oz. Ditalini
2 medium acorn squash (about 1 1/2 lb. ea.),
   split, peeled, seeded, and quartered
2 tbsp. margarine
1 large onion, chopped
1 c. grated carrot
1 1/2 tsp. brown sugar
3/4 tsp. ground mace or nutmeg
1/2 tsp. ground ginger
1/2 tsp. cinnamon
3 cans (13 1/4 oz. ea.) low-sodium chicken
   broth (about 6 cups)
1 c. non-fat sour cream
1 tbsp. sugar

Cook squash in one inch of water in covered saucepan for 15 minutes or until tender. Cool. Scrape out pulp and put back in pot. Add margarine, onion, carrot, sugar, mace, ginger, and cinnamon. Cover and simmer gently for 10 minutes, stirring occasionally. Cook until vegetables are tender.

Add half of broth to squash mixture and purée all in a blender or food processor. Return to pot and add remaining broth. Bring to a boil and add pasta. Cook, stirring occasionally, for 10 minutes or until pasta is done.

Before serving, blend sour cream and sugar in a separate bowl. Put dollop on top of each bowl of soup. Serve hot.

Pasta With Roasted Vegetables

8 oz. rigatoni, mostaccioli, or other
  medium pasta shape
1 lb. fresh mixed vegetables, such as green beans,
  red onions, snow peas, asparagus, carrots, squash,
  turnips, zucchini, leeks, fennel, red or green bell
  peppers, mushrooms
salt and pepper to taste
1 tsp. Italian seasoning
2 tbsp. vegetable or olive oil
2 tsp. balsamic vinegar
1/4 c. chicken broth
2 tbsp. Parmesan cheese, grated

Preheat oven to 500°F. Prepare pasta according to
package directions. While pasta is cooking, slice or
cut vegetables and place in a single layer in a
shallow baking dish. Season with salt, pepper, and
Italian seasoning; brush lightly with oil. Roast in
oven for about 10 minutes or until vegetables
caramelize and brown, leaving any juice on baking
dish. Drain and set juices aside. Chop vegetables
into 1-inch pieces.

When pasta is done, drain well. Toss cooked pasta
with vegetable juice, vegetables, vinegar, chicken
broth, and Parmesan cheese. Serve immediately.

Green and White Lasagne

6 pieces lasagna
1/2 c. onion, chopped
2 tbsp. butter
2 tbsp. cornstarch
1 tbsp. dried parsley flakes
1 tsp. dried basil, crushed
1/4 tsp. garlic powder
1/8 tsp. ground nutmeg
2 c. skim milk
1 pkg. (10 oz.) frozen chopped spinach,
  thawed and drained
1 can (2 1/4 oz.) sliced pitted ripe olives, drained
1 carton (15 oz.) part-skim ricotta cheese
1 egg, beaten

1 pkg. (8 oz.) mozzarella cheese, shredded
1/2 c. Parmesan cheese, grated

Cook lasagna according to package directions;
drain. Rinse in cold water; drain well. In a
medium saucepan, cook onion in butter until
tender. Stir in cornstarch, parsley, basil, garlic
powder, and nutmeg. Add milk all at once. Cook
and stir until thickened and bubbly. Stir in spinach
and olives.

In a medium bowl, stir together ricotta and egg.
Add mozzarella and half of Parmesan; mix well.

Preheat oven to 350° F. Arrange three lasagna
pieces in bottom of a greased 12x7x2-inch baking
dish. Top with half of spinach mixture and half
ricotta mixture. Repeat layers. Top with remaining
Parmesan cheese. Bake for 40 minutes or until
mixture is bubbly. Let stand 10 minutes.

Penne With Zucchini And Parmesan

1 lb. penne, mostaccioli, or other
  medium pasta shape
1 lb. zucchini
2 tbsp. butter
1 tbsp. olive or vegetable oil
1 large clove garlic, minced
1/4 tsp. hot red pepper flakes
2/3 c. fresh Parmesan cheese, grated

Cook pasta according to package directions.
While pasta is cooking, grate zucchini. Heat butter
and oil together in large skillet until mixture
begins to bubble. Add grated zucchini and cook
about 3 minutes. Add garlic and cook 1 more
minute, stirring constantly. Stir in hot pepper
flakes and 2/3 cup of grated Parmesan cheese.
Heat 1 minute more. When pasta is done, drain
well. Toss skillet mixture with pasta. Top with
additional Parmesan, if desired.

Pasta Salads

Shred:

To rub on a shredder to form long, narrow pieces.

Stir:

To mix ingredients with a spoon using a circular motion.

Creamy Pesto Pasta Salad

1 7-oz. pkg. refrigerated prepared pesto
1/2 c. salad dressing
3 c. Rotini, cooked and drained
1/4 c. ripe olives, pitted and sliced
3 tbsp. sun-dried tomatoes in oil, drained
  and chopped
1 tsp. ground black pepper

Combine pesto and salad dressing in a large
bowl until well combined. Stir in remaining
ingredients. Refrigerate 1 hour or until ready to
serve.

Tangy Pasta Salad

6 slices bacon
1 1/4 c. salad dressing
2 tbsp. sugar
1/2 tsp. garlic salt
1 16-oz. pkg. macaroni, cooked and drained
3 carrots, shredded
1 green pepper, chopped
1 red onion, sliced

Fry bacon in skillet on medium heat to desired
crispness. Drain bacon, reserving 2 tablespoons
drippings. Crumble bacon and set aside.
Combine reserved bacon drippings, dressing,
sugar, and garlic salt in large bowl. Add all
remaining ingredients except bacon. Toss
lightly and refrigerate. Sprinkle with crumbled
bacon before serving.

Macaroni Salad

1 10 3/4-oz. can cream of celery soup
3/4 c. mayonnaise
3 tbsp. vinegar
1/2 tsp. black pepper
4 c. elbow macaroni, cooked
2 stalks celery, chopped
1 small green pepper, chopped

2 green onions, chopped
2 hard-boiled eggs, chopped

Combine soup, mayonnaise, vinegar and black
pepper. Add macaroni, celery, green pepper,
onions and eggs. Toss ingredients to coat.
Cover; refrigerate at least 6 hours or overnight.

Chicken Pasta Salad

1 (14 1/2-oz.) can chicken broth
1/2 c. mayonnaise
1/4 c. Parmesan cheese
1 tsp. dried basil leaves, crushed
3 c. Rotini, cooked and hot
1 c. cherry tomatoes, cut in half
1 c. frozen peas
1/2 c. mushrooms, sliced
1 small red onion, chopped
2 c. chicken, cooked and cubed
lettuce leaves

In medium bowl mix broth, mayonnaise, cheese,
and basil. In large, shallow, non-metallic dish,
toss Rotini, tomatoes, peas, mushrooms, onion,
chicken, and broth mixture until evenly coated.
Refrigerate at least 4 hours or overnight, stirring
occasionally. Serve on lettuce.

Bistro Chicken Pasta Salad

2 c. penne pasta, cooked
1 c. cherry tomatoes, quartered
3/4 c. feta cheese, crumbled
1/2 c. honey mustard dressing
1/3 c. lightly packed fresh basil leaves,
  cut into strips
1/4 c. red onion, chopped
1/4 c. sun-dried tomatoes, chopped
2 chicken breast halves, broiled; cut into
  1/4-inch slices

Combine all ingredients except chicken. Mix
pasta mixture with chicken. Serve warm or
chilled.

Ravioli Salad

1/4 c. olive oil
2 tbsp. red wine vinegar
1 1/2 tsp. dried rosemary
1 large garlic clove, minced
1 tsp. sugar
1/2 tsp. dried red pepper, crushed
1 9-oz. pkg. cheese ravioli, freshly cooked
1 1/2 c. diced ham
1 red bell pepper, diced
1 small jar mushrooms, drained
4 green onions, chopped
Parmesan cheese, grated

Whisk together first 6 ingredients in large bowl. Wash ravioli under cold water to cool and drain. Combine ravioli, ham, bell pepper, mushrooms, and green onions with oil mixture and toss to coat. Season salad with salt and pepper to taste. Cover and chill at least 30 minutes. Sprinkle Parmesan cheese to taste on each individual serving.

Dressed-Up Pasta and Pepper Salad

2 1/2 c. Rotini
1 medium zucchini, thinly sliced
1 medium carrot, thinly sliced
1 small green bell pepper, chopped
1 small red bell pepper, chopped
1 can pitted ripe olives, drained
1/2 c. crumbled feta cheese
1/4 tsp. red pepper, crushed
1 c. Italian salad dressing

Combine all ingredients except dressing in large bowl. Pour in dressing and toss to coat. Cover and refrigerate at least 1 hour before serving.

Blue Cheese Pasta Salad

8 oz. macaroni, uncooked
4 oz. blue cheese, crumbled
2 c. walnuts, chopped
1 c. celery, chopped
4 tbsp. mayonnaise
1/8 tsp. white pepper
1/8 tsp. salt
3 tbsp. parsley, minced

Prepare pasta according to package directions. Rinse with cold water and drain well.

Add all ingredients to pasta and gently toss until all ingredients are well mixed. Refrigerate until ready to serve.

Sprinkle with parsley and serve slightly chilled.

Shell Salad

4 oz. pasta shells
1 15-oz. can red kidney beans, rinsed
  and drained
1 12-oz. can corn, drained
4 green onions, finely chopped
4 green chilies, finely chopped
1/2 tsp. ground cumin
1 tsp. dried oregano
1 tbsp. lemon juice
1/2 c. mayonnaise
1 tsp. salt
1/2 tsp. ground pepper

Prepare pasta according to package directions. Rinse with cold water and drain thoroughly.

Combine all ingredients in large serving bowl. Toss gently until mixed thoroughly. Chill for at least 2 hours before serving.

Double-Decker Pasta Salad

8 oz. elbow macaroni
2 c. fresh green beans, cut in half
1 c. plain, low-fat yogurt
1 tbsp. Dijon mustard
2 tbsp. honey
2 medium carrots, grated
1 red apple, diced (about 1 1/4 c.)
1 can (6 1/8-oz.) white tuna packed
  in water, drained
1/4 c. chopped walnuts
1/2 c. cheddar cheese, grated

Prepare pasta according to package directions; drain. Blanch green beans by cooking in pot of boiling water for 2 minutes. Drain and rinse well with cold water. Drain again.

Combine yogurt, Dijon mustard, and honey in blender or food processor. Mix well and set aside. Spread half of cooked pasta in bottom of a 3-quart glass bowl, trifle dish or glass baking dish.

Top with half each of green beans, carrots, apple, and tuna. Drizzle half of dressing evenly over salad. Repeat with remaining ingredients. Sprinkle top with walnuts and cheddar cheese. Cover and chill for 30 minutes. Serve cold.

Orange Pasta Salad with Light Orange Vinaigrette

1 lb. medium shells, elbow macaroni,
  or other medium pasta shape
3 c. boneless and skinless chicken breasts,
  cooked and cooled
1 1/4 c. red or white seedless grapes, cut in half
1 large cucumber, peeled, seeded and
  cut into chunks
6 scallions, sliced
3 c. navel oranges, peeled and sectioned
1 head of lettuce

Light Orange Vinaigrette
1/4 c. vegetable oil
1/4 c. white wine vinegar
3/4 c. orange juice concentrate
1 tsp. salt
1/2 tsp. pepper

Prepare pasta according to package directions; drain. Cut chicken into 1-inch cubes. In a large mixing bowl, stir together pasta, chicken, grapes, cucumber, scallions and half of orange sections. In a small mixing bowl, whisk together all vinaigrette ingredients. Pour vinaigrette into pasta mixture and toss salad gently. On a large platter, arrange lettuce leaves. Mound salad on top of lettuce and garnish with remaining orange slices.

Pasta and Beef Salad

1 lb. Orzo, small shells, or other small pasta shape
2 c. deli roast beef, cubed
3 medium ripe tomatoes, chopped
1 c. zucchini, chopped
1 c. fresh parsley, chopped
1/2 c. green onion, chopped fine
2 tbsp. fresh mint, minced
3 cloves garlic, minced
1/2 c. lemon juice
2 tbsp. olive or vegetable oil
1 tsp. black pepper
salt to taste

Prepare pasta according to package directions. Drain and rinse under cold water; drain again. In a large mixing bowl, combine pasta, beef, tomatoes, zucchini, parsley, onion, and mint. In a small mixing bowl, combine remaining ingredients; whisk well. Toss dressing with pasta mixture. Salt to taste. Serve immediately or refrigerate until ready to serve.

Pasta and Walnut Fruit Salad

8 oz. medium shells, Rotini or other
    medium pasta shape
1 c. non-fat, plain yogurt
1 tbsp. honey
1/4 c. frozen orange juice concentrate, thawed
1 can (11 oz.) juice-packed mandarin
    oranges, drained
1 c. seedless red grapes, cut into halves
1 c. seedless green grapes, cut into halves
1 apple, cored and chopped
1/2 c. celery, sliced
1/2 c. walnut halves

Prepare pasta according to package directions;
drain. In a small bowl, blend yogurt, honey, and
orange juice concentrate. In a large bowl, combine
pasta and remaining ingredients. Add yogurt
mixture; toss to coat. Cover and chill thoroughly.

Radiatore Salad With Salmon and Papaya

1 lb. Radiatore
6 tbsp. vegetable oil
fresh ground black pepper to taste
1 lb. skinless and boneless, fresh or frozen
    salmon fillets, cooked and chopped, or 2 cans
    (7 1/2 oz. ea.) salmon, drained and flaked
1 papaya, peeled, seeded and chopped
1 c. cherry tomatoes
1 bunch scallions, sliced fine
1 yellow bell pepper, seeded, ribs removed,
    and chopped
1 medium cucumber, quartered lengthwise
    and sliced
1 small jalapeño, seeded, ribs removed,
    and minced fine
2 tbsp. fresh cilantro, chopped or 2 tsp.
    dried cilantro

3 tbsp. rice wine vinegar
3 tbsp. white wine vinegar
3 drops hot sauce

Prepare pasta according to package directions;
drain and transfer to a medium bowl. While
pasta is still warm, mix in vegetable oil. Season
with black pepper. Set pasta aside to cool.

In a medium mixing bowl, add salmon, papaya,
tomatoes, scallions, yellow pepper, and
cucumber. Toss together with pasta.

In a small bowl, combine jalapeño, cilantro,
both vinegars, and hot sauce. Toss pasta with
dressing and refrigerate. Chill well before
serving.

Rigatoni-Turkey Salad

8 oz. Rigatoni
1 1/2 c. turkey, cubed and cooked
1/4 c. onion, chopped
1 c. carrots, sliced thin
1 c. frozen peas, thawed
2 tbsp. vegetable oil
2 tbsp. cider vinegar
1/4 tsp. thyme
1/4 tsp. salt
1/4 tsp. pepper

Prepare pasta according to package directions,
drain and rinse with cold water. Drain well.

Combine turkey and vegetables in a large
bowl. Add pasta. Combine oil, vinegar and
seasonings in a jar. Shake well to blend. Pour
over pasta and stir well. Cover and chill until
ready to serve.

Shrimp and Feta Cheese Salad

1 lb. small shells, Ditalini, or other
  small pasta shape
2 tbsp. butter
2 tbsp. flour
2 c. milk
2 medium tomatoes, chopped
1 c. feta cheese, cubed
1 lb. small shrimp, cooked
1 green bell pepper, chopped
1/2 c. drained black olives, pitted and sliced
1 tbsp. parsley, chopped
2 cloves garlic, minced
1 tsp. oregano
1 tsp. salt
1/2 tsp. black pepper

Topping

1/2 c. almonds, sliced
1/4 c. fresh bread crumbs
1/4 c. Parmesan cheese, grated
2 tbsp. butter, melted

Prepare pasta according to package directions; drain. Melt margarine in saucepan; whisk in flour. Cook until mixture is bubbly. Whisk in milk. Cook over medium-low heat for 20 minutes, stirring often. Toss together pasta, sauce, and all remaining ingredients except topping. Spoon mixture into a 2 1/2-quart casserole dish. Cover and bake at 350° F for 20 minutes.

While pasta is baking, toss together almonds, bread crumbs and Parmesan cheese. Mix in butter. When pasta is done, remove from oven, sprinkle topping over pasta and serve.

Springtime Pasta Salad

12 oz. spaghetti, linguine, or thin spaghetti
1 tbsp. vegetable oil
8 oz. broccoli florets
8 oz. asparagus, cut into 1-inch pieces
4 scallions or spring onions, cut into 1-inch slices
2 cloves garlic, chopped fine
1 pkg. (10 oz.) frozen peas, thawed and drained
1 green or red bell pepper, chopped coarse
8 oz. mushrooms, sliced
1/4 c. fresh parsley, minced

Dressing

3 tbsp. red wine vinegar
3 tbsp. fresh lemon juice
1 tbsp. Dijon mustard
1/2 tsp. basil
1/2 tsp. oregano
1/2 tsp. thyme
1/8 tsp. cayenne pepper
2 tbsp. vegetable oil
fresh ground black pepper to taste

Prepare pasta according to package directions; drain. Toss with vegetable oil to keep pasta from sticking.

In a large pot, cook broccoli and asparagus in boiling water until crisp yet tender, about 4 minutes. Drain and add to pasta. Add scallions, garlic, peas, bell pepper, mushrooms, and parsley to pasta.

In a small bowl, whisk together first seven dressing ingredients. Slowly whisk in oil until dressing is well blended. Season with pepper.

Pour dressing over pasta mixture and toss gently until well mixed.

Ethnic Dishes

Stir-Fry:
To cook quickly in a small amount of fat, stirring constantly.

Toss:
To mix ingredients lightly by lifting and dropping
with a spoon, or a spoon and a fork.

Mandarin Chicken Pasta

1 c. salad dressing
1/2 c. orange juice
2 tsp. dried basil leaves
1/4 tsp. ground ginger
4 boneless and skinless chicken breast
    halves, cooked and cubed
2 c. Rotini, cooked and drained
1 11-oz. can mandarin orange
    segments, drained
1/2 c. pecans, chopped

Mix salad dressing, juice, and seasonings in
large bowl. Add remaining ingredients and toss
lightly. Refrigerate until ready to serve.

Chinese Pasta Salad with Tuna

2 c. macaroni
2 (6 1/8-oz.) cans white tuna in water, flaked
3/4 c. water chestnuts, sliced and drained
1 c. salad dressing
1 c. broccoli florets
1 c. carrots, chopped
1 c. celery, sliced
1 tsp. dill weed
1/2 tsp. black pepper, ground
1 c. Chinese noodles

Prepare pasta according to package directions;
drain. Combine pasta with remaining
ingredients. Chill for two hours; sprinkle with
Chinese noodles and serve.

Italian Pasta Salad

2 c. large bowtie pasta
1 1/2 c. cherry tomatoes, halved
1 c. cucumber slices, halved
1 c. mushrooms, sliced
1/2 c. salami strips
1/2 c. Italian dressing
1 c. sour cream
1/4 c. Parmesan cheese, grated
1/4 c. green onions, sliced

Cook pasta according to package directions;
drain. In a large bowl combine tomatoes,
cucumber, mushrooms, meat, and pasta; pour
dressing over mixture. Cover and refrigerate
2 hours or overnight to marinate. Just before
serving, combine sour cream, Parmesan cheese,
and onions; toss with pasta mixture.

Quick and Easy Chop Suey

1 lb. ground beef
1 large onion, sliced
1 c. carrots, sliced
1 c. celery, sliced
1 c. rice, cooked
1/4 stick margarine
salt and pepper to taste

Brown ground beef in heavy skillet. Stir in
remaining ingredients. Cook slowly until carrots
are tender, about 30 minutes.

Mexicali Beef Salsa Macaroni

1 lb. ground beef
1 16-oz. jar chunky salsa
1 1/2 c. water
1 pkg. macaroni and cheese dinner
1/2 c. salad dressing

Brown meat and drain. Stir in salsa, water,
uncooked macaroni, dry cheese sauce mix, and
dressing. Stir until thoroughly mixed. Bring
mixture to a boil. Reduce heat to low. Cover and
simmer 7 minutes or until macaroni is tender,
stirring occasionally. Remove from heat. Let
stand, covered, 5 minutes and then serve.

Cheesy Tex-Mex Chili-Mac

2 lb. ground beef
1 c. onion, chopped
1 14 1/2-oz. can tomatoes, diced and undrained
1 15-oz. can kidney beans, rinsed and drained
1 can tomato paste
1/2 c. water
3 tbsp. chili powder
2 tsp. ground cumin
1 jar processed cheese sauce
4 c. macaroni, cooked and hot

Brown meat with onion in a large sauce pan on medium-high heat. Drain and return to pot. Reduce heat to medium-low and add tomatoes, beans, tomato paste, water, chili powder and cumin. Cover and simmer 10 minutes or until thoroughly heated. Stir in cheese sauce until melted. Spoon over prepared macaroni.

Italian Soup

1 tbsp. olive oil
1 green bell pepper, diced
1 small onion, chopped
3 large garlic cloves, chopped
1 tbsp. dried basil
1 tsp. fennel seeds
1/2 tsp. dried red pepper, crushed
6 c. chicken broth
2 medium zucchini, diced
1 carrot, diced
1 9-oz. package fresh cheese ravioli
1 1/2 c. cooked chicken, diced
salt and pepper to taste
Parmesan cheese, grated

Heat oil in large, heavy saucepan over medium heat. Sauté bell pepper, onion, garlic, basil, fennel seeds, and red pepper until tender, about 10 minutes. Stir in chicken broth. Cover pot and simmer 10 minutes. Add zucchini and carrot; cover. Simmer until carrot is almost tender, about 15 minutes.

Increase heat to high and bring soup to boil. Add ravioli and boil until tender, about 5 minutes. Add chicken and cook until just heated through, about 5 minutes. Season soup to taste with salt and pepper. Sprinkle Parmesan cheese over each individual serving.

Oriental Pepper Steak

1 lb. chuck roast, cut into 1-inch strips
1 tsp. salt
1/4 c. oil
2 tbsp. soy sauce
1 garlic clove, minced
1 1/2 c. water, divided
1 c. green pepper, cut in strips
1 large onion, sliced
1/2 c. celery, sliced
1/2 c. mushrooms
2 tomatoes, cut in wedges
1 tbsp. cornstarch
4 c. rice, cooked and hot

Massage meat with salt and brown quickly in hot oil. Add soy sauce, garlic, and 1/2 cup water. Bring to a boil and decrease heat, simmering 45 minutes or until meat is tender. Stir in green pepper, onion, celery, and mushrooms.

Cover and simmer until vegetables are tender-crisp. Add tomato wedges and lightly toss. Dissolve cornstarch in 1 cup of water and stir into meat mixture. Cook over medium heat, stirring constantly, until mixture boils and thickens. Serve over hot rice.

Asian Chicken Pasta

4 tbsp. soy sauce
2 tbsp. honey
2 tbsp. lime juice
3 tsp. Dijon mustard
1 lb. boneless and skinless chicken breast
  meat, cubed
1/2 c. chicken broth
1 lb. mostaccioli, uncooked
2 small red bell peppers, thinly sliced
6 scallions, thinly sliced
pepper, freshly ground

Stir soy sauce, honey, lime juice and mustard in a small bowl until honey is dissolved. Add chicken pieces and turn until coated with marinade. Refrigerate for 30 minutes.

Transfer chicken and marinade to a large, non-stick skillet. Cook over medium heat until chicken is cooked through, about 4 minutes. Remove from heat and add chicken broth.

Prepare pasta according to package directions; drain. Return pasta to pot; add contents of skillet, red peppers, and scallions. Heat to simmering over low heat. Toss pasta and add pepper to taste.

Spanish Rice

1 c. water
3/4 c. green pepper
1/2 c. onion, chopped
1/2 c. celery
1/2 tsp. salt
1 (14 1/2-oz.) can tomatoes, cut up
3/4 c. long grain rice
1 tsp. chili powder
1/8 tsp. pepper
dash hot pepper sauce

In a medium saucepan combine water, green pepper, onion, celery, and salt. Bring to a boil. Reduce heat and cover, simmering for 5 minutes. Stir in undrained tomatoes, rice, chili powder, pepper, and hot pepper sauce. Return to boiling and reduce heat. Cover and simmer about 20 minutes or until rice is tender and liquid is absorbed.

Mexican Pasta Casserole

1 lb. ziti
2 tsp. vegetable oil
1 medium chopped onion
1 minced garlic clove
1 jalapeño, seeded and minced
3 tbsp. chili powder
1 28-oz. can diced tomatoes, undrained
1 tsp. cumin
1 tsp. dried oregano
8 oz. boneless and skinless chicken breast
  meat, cooked and cubed
1 c. Monterey Jack cheese, grated and divided

Preheat oven to 375°F. Prepare pasta according to package directions; drain well.

Meanwhile, heat oil in a medium saucepan over medium heat. Add onion, garlic, and jalapeño; cook until softened, about 3 minutes. Add chili powder and stir for 1 minute. Add tomatoes and liquid, cumin, and oregano. Simmer until slightly thickened, about 15 minutes.

Combine pasta, chicken, 3/4 cup cheese, and sauce in a large bowl. Spoon into a 2-quart baking dish which has been lightly sprayed with vegetable oil. Sprinkle reserved cheese on top. Cover loosely with foil and bake until warmed through and cheese is melted, about 15 minutes.

Chinese Noodle Salad

1/4 c. sesame seeds
1/2 lb. dried Chinese noodles
2 tbsp. vegetable oil
1 bunch broccoli, cut into 1-inch florets
1 lb. asparagus, cut on the diagonal
  into 1-inch pieces
1/2 c. chicken broth
1/2 c. peanut butter
1/4 c. red wine vinegar
2 tbsp. soy sauce
1 tbsp. sesame oil
1 tbsp. dry sherry
2 tsp. sugar
1 1/2 tsp. Chinese chili sauce
2 tbsp. fresh ginger, finely minced
1 clove garlic, minced
1 c. bean sprouts
1 c. mushrooms, thinly sliced
1 large red bell pepper, cut into
  match-sized strips
2 tbsp. chives, minced

In a small, dry skillet, toast sesame seeds over moderately high heat until fragrant and golden brown, about 1 minute.

In a large pot of boiling salted water, cook noodles until tender but still firm, about 2 1/2 minutes. Rinse with cold water and drain well. Toss with vegetable oil.

Bring a large saucepan of salted water to a boil over high heat. Add broccoli and cook until tender-crisp, 2 to 3 minutes. Using a slotted spoon, transfer broccoli to a bowl of ice water and chill until cold, about 5 minutes. Drain on paper towels. Repeat with asparagus, cooking for only 1 to 2 minutes.

In a small saucepan, bring stock to boil over moderately high heat. Once boiling, remove from heat and add peanut butter, vinegar, soy sauce, sesame oil, sherry, sugar, chili sauce, ginger, garlic, and toasted sesame seeds.

In a large bowl, toss together noodles, broccoli, asparagus, bean sprouts, mushrooms, and red pepper. Add dressing and toss to coat. Sprinkle chives over top and serve.

Pasta Chili

1 lb. elbow macaroni
1 lb. ground beef
3 tbsp. vegetable oil
1 28-oz. can tomatoes with juice
1 qt. tomato juice
2 c. onions, chopped
3 cloves garlic, minced
1 tsp. salt
1 tbsp. chili powder
1 tsp. ground cumin
1 tsp. dried oregano
1 tsp. pepper
1 bay leaf
1 20-oz. can red kidney beans, drained

Cook pasta according to package directions; drain. In a large skillet brown beef in oil, stirring frequently. Add undrained tomatoes, tomato juice, onions, garlic, salt, and remaining seasonings. Cover and simmer for 45 minutes. Stir in kidney beans and cook for an additional 30 minutes. Discard bay leaf. Gradually stir in cooked pasta; serve.

Japanese Orange Fettuccine

12 oz. fettuccine
1 8-oz. can orange juice concentrate
5 tbsp. teriyaki sauce
2 tbsp. lime juice
12 oz. boneless and skinless chicken
  breast meat
1 8-oz. can water chestnuts, sliced and drained
3 tbsp. pecans, chopped and lightly toasted
2 bunches watercress, coarsely chopped

Prepare pasta according to package directions; drain well.

Meanwhile, stir together orange juice concentrate, teriyaki sauce, and lime juice in a skillet over medium heat. Add chicken and cover, simmering for 4 minutes. Turn chicken; cover and cook for 4 more minutes or until done. Remove chicken to a cutting board and let it cool.

Add water chestnuts to orange sauce. Bring to a boil and stir. Slice chicken into strips and add to sauce. In a large serving bowl, toss together hot pasta, pecans, and watercress. Add chicken and orange sauce; serve.

Irish Lasagne

6 pieces lasagna, uncooked
1/2 c. onion, chopped
2 tbsp. margarine
2 tbsp. cornstarch
1 tbsp. dried parsley flakes
1 tsp. dried basil
1/4 tsp. garlic powder
1/8 tsp. ground nutmeg
2 c. milk
1 10-oz. package frozen spinach, chopped,
thawed and drained
15 oz. ricotta cheese
1 egg, beaten
8 oz. mozzarella cheese, shredded
1/2 c. Parmesan cheese, grated

Preheat oven to 350°F. Cook lasagna according to package directions; rinse in cold water and drain thoroughly.

In a medium saucepan, cook onion in margarine until tender. Stir in cornstarch, parsley, basil, garlic powder, and nutmeg. Add milk all at once. Cook and stir until thickened and bubbly. Stir in spinach.

In a medium bowl, stir together ricotta and egg. Add mozzarella and half of Parmesan; mix well.

Arrange three lasagna pieces in bottom of a greased 12x7x2-inch baking dish. Top with half of spinach mixture and half of ricotta mixture. Repeat layers. Top with remaining Parmesan cheese. Bake for 40 minutes or until mixture is bubbly. Let stand 10 minutes.

Japanese Pasta

1 lb. spaghetti or linguine
12-16 oz. flank steak, cut on diagonal
  (across grain of meat) into thin strips
1/3 c. low-sodium soy sauce
1 red bell pepper, halved and sliced
2 carrots, sliced into 1/4-inch rounds
2 bunches scallions, sliced

Prepare pasta according to package directions; drain. In a nonstick skillet, sauté flank steak over high heat. If it begins to stick, add a little soy sauce, one tablespoon at a time. When the steak is cooked through, reduce heat to medium-low and add soy sauce, red bell pepper, carrots, and scallions. Increase heat to medium-high and cook 3 minutes. Toss with pasta and serve.

Chinese Pasta Salad

1 1/2 c. snow peas
8 1/2 oz. vermicelli noodles
1 red pepper, sliced thin
1/2 English cucumber, sliced thin
6 oz. shrimp, cooked
4 1/2 oz. crabmeat
1 tbsp. fresh ginger, chopped fine
1 clove garlic, chopped
2 tbsp. sesame oil
1/2 tsp. black pepper
1 1/2 tsp. salt
3 tsp. vegetable oil
2 tbsp. lemon juice
1 tsp. red wine vinegar

Wash and trim snow peas. Place them in a bowl and pour in enough boiling water to cover them. Let stand 10 minutes; drain and set aside.

Cook noodles in plenty of boiling water for 3-4 minutes. Drain in colander, rinse with cold water, and set aside.

In large bowl, combine noodles, snow peas, red pepper, cucumber, shrimp, and crabmeat.

In a small bowl, combine ginger, garlic, sesame oil, pepper, salt, vegetable oil, lemon juice, and vinegar.

Pour this dressing over other ingredients and mix thoroughly.

Chill before serving.

Pasta With Chinese Tahini Sauce

8 oz. pasta (preferably buckwheat noodles or Chinese wheat noodles)
1 c. peas
scallion curls, fresh coriander sprigs, toasted sesame seeds, or chopped dry-roasted unsalted peanuts for garnish (optional)

Chinese Tahini Sauce

2 tbsp. Tahini (sesame butter)
2 tsp. hot chili paste with garlic
1 tbsp. rice vinegar
1 tsp. minced ginger root
1 tbsp. soy sauce
2 tbsp. vegetable stock or water
1 tbsp. sesame oil
1 dash freshly ground black pepper

Bring a large pot of water to a boil; cook pasta until *al dente*. (If using Chinese wheat noodles: break compacted cubes and drop into boiling water. When water returns to a boil, cook for 3 minutes; drain. Served as is or pat dry and sautée in oil until lightly browned.)

While pasta is cooking, steam peas. In a large bowl, combine ingredients for Tahini sauce. When pasta is done, drain well. Toss sauce with pasta; add peas and toss again. Garnish as desired.

VARIATIONS: Sauté 6 ounces chopped spinach in 1 tablespoon safflower oil until limp; add mushrooms, blanched pea pods, sweet red peppers, steamed broccoli, steamed sliced carrots, or scallions. If you add several, the amount of dressing may need to be increased.

Mexican Pasta Pie

1/2 onion, finely chopped
1 can (28 oz.) tomatoes with juice,
  coarsely chopped
1 (1-1/4 oz.) package taco seasoning
1 can (16 oz.) black beans, rinsed and drained
1 3/4 c. dried pasta
2 tsp. olive oil
4 c. ziti or penne pasta, cooked
1 c. part-skim ricotta
2 (8 oz.) boneless and skinless chicken
  breast halves, cut into 1/2-inch pieces
1 c. cheddar or Mexican blend cheese, shredded

Preheat oven to 425°F. Grease a 7x11-inch baking dish. In a medium bowl, mix onions, tomatoes, taco seasoning, and black beans. Toss dried pasta with olive oil and add to tomato mixture.

Spread 1 cup tomato mixture on bottom of baking dish. Add cooked pasta. Dot with ricotta and spread with a knife. Stir chicken pieces into remaining tomato mixture and spoon over ricotta. Sprinkle with shredded cheese. Bake 25-30 minutes. Serve immediately.

VARIATION: Omit chicken to make a vegetarian meal.

Asian Chicken Pasta Salad

8 oz. Orzo, small shells, or other small pasta shape
2 c. chicken, poached and cut into chunks
4 oz. spinach leaves, stems removed and
  sliced into strips
1/2 c. bean sprouts
1/2 red bell pepper, ribs removed and cut into strips
2 scallions, sliced
3 tbsp. red wine vinegar
1 tbsp. reduced-sodium soy sauce
1 tbsp. sesame or vegetable oil
2 tsp. teriyaki sauce
1 1/2 tbsp. prepared chili sauce
1 tbsp. fresh ginger, grated
3 tbsp. slivered almonds, toasted

Prepare pasta according to package directions; drain.

In large mixing bowl combine pasta, chicken, spinach, sprouts, pepper, and scallions. In a small mixing bowl, combine all remaining ingredients except almonds; whisk well. Toss dressing with pasta mixture and refrigerate until ready to serve. Sprinkle almonds over top just before serving.

Mediterranean Fettuccine With Shrimp and Spinach

12 oz. fettuccine
1 c. plain, non-fat yogurt
1/2 c. feta cheese, crumbled
2 cloves garlic, minced
1 tbsp. chopped fresh dill or 1 tsp. dried dill
1/2 tsp. freshly ground black pepper
12 oz. medium frozen shrimp, thawed
1 pkg. (10-oz.) frozen chopped spinach, thawed
salt to taste

Prepare pasta according to package directions. While the pasta is cooking, stir together yogurt, feta cheese, garlic, dill, and pepper in a large mixing bowl.

Two minutes before pasta is done, stir shrimp and spinach into pot with pasta. Cook 2 minutes.

Drain pasta, shrimp, and spinach thoroughly. Stir into yogurt mixture and season to taste with salt. Serve immediately.

Pasta Classics

Zest:
To remove the outmost skin of citrus fruit with a knife, peeler, or zester. Be careful not to remove the pith (the white layer between the zest and the flesh), which is very bitter.

Drizzle:
To pour a liquid, such as butter or melted chocolate, over food in a thin stream.

Lasagna Casserole

1 16-oz. pkg. wide egg noodles
1 lb. ground pork
salt, pepper and garlic to taste
1 onion, sliced
1 1/2 c. cottage cheese
1/2 c. Parmesan cheese
1 jar spaghetti sauce
2 c. cheddar cheese, grated

Preheat oven to 425°F. Boil noodles until soft, then drain. Place cooked noodles in bottom of buttered 13x9-inch casserole dish.

Fry ground pork thoroughly, seasoning with salt, pepper, and garlic. Add onion and fry until tender, 2-3 minutes. Layer pork mixture over noodles. Spread cottage cheese over pork and onions. Sprinkle on Parmesan cheese. Pour spaghetti sauce over all. Top with cheddar cheese. Bake until cheese is melted and casserole is bubbly.

Spicy Macaroni 'n Cheese

1 pkg. macaroni and cheese dinner
2 tbsp. butter
1 onion, chopped
1 green bell pepper, chopped
2 tomatoes, chopped
1 tbsp. dried tomatoes, chopped
1 green onion, chopped

Boil macaroni for 10 minutes and drain. Heat butter and sauté onion for 1 minute. Add bell pepper and tomatoes. Stir-fry for 5 minutes. Add macaroni and cheese; sprinkle with green onion.

Tasty Spaghetti in White Sauce

1 10.5-oz. pkg. spaghetti
2 c. mushrooms
1/2 stick plus 1 tbsp. butter
1 c. milk, divided
2 egg yolks
6 strips bacon
1/4 c. white wine
3/4 c. whipping cream
2 oz. Parmesan cheese

Cook pasta according to package directions. Meanwhile, sauté mushrooms in 1 tablespoon butter; set aside. Add 1/2 cup milk to egg yolks; set aside. Cook bacon and drain. Add white wine and 1/2 stick butter; stir. When butter is melted, add mushrooms. Simmer for about 10 minutes. Add whipping cream, Parmesan cheese, and pasta. Simmer another 5 minutes; add milk and egg yolks. Cook until cream is thickened. Serve immediately.

Easy Lasagne

1 jar prepared spaghetti sauce, divided
6 dry lasagna noodles
15 oz. ricotta cheese
2 c. mozzarella cheese, shredded and divided
1/4 c. Parmesan cheese, grated

In 2-quart shallow baking dish, spread 1 cup spaghetti sauce. Top with 3 lasagna noodles, ricotta cheese, 1 cup mozzarella cheese, Parmesan cheese and 1 cup spaghetti sauce. Top with remaining 3 lasagna noodles and remaining spaghetti sauce. Cover. Bake at 375°F for 1 hour. Uncover and top with remaining mozzarella cheese. Let stand 5 minutes.

Classic Baked Mostaccioli

1 lb. ground beef
4 c. mostaccioli, cooked and drained
1 jar spaghetti sauce
3/4 c. Romano cheese, divided
2 c. mozzarella cheese, shredded

Preheat oven to 375°F. Meanwhile, brown meat in large skillet; drain. Stir in cooked pasta, spaghetti sauce, and 1/2 cup Romano cheese. Pour into 13x9-inch baking dish. Top with mozzarella cheese and remaining 1/4 cup Romano cheese. Bake for 20 minutes.

Feta Fettuccine

12 oz. fettuccine
3 tbsp. olive oil
8 oz. feta cheese
2 c. chopped tomatoes
1 1/2 tsp. dried basil
fresh ground black pepper to taste

Cook fettuccine 8 to 10 minutes; drain and return to pan. Toss with olive oil, feta cheese, tomatoes, and basil. Season to taste with pepper.

Easy Macaroni 'n Cheese

1/2 lb. process cheese spread, cubed
1/4 c. milk
1 c. elbow macaroni, cooked and drained
dash ground black pepper

Preheat oven to 350°F. Melt process cheese spread and milk in saucepan on low heat until smooth. Add macaroni and pepper. Spoon into 1-quart casserole and bake for 20 minutes.

Quick Baked Ziti

16 oz. ziti, cooked and drained
2 c. tomato sauce
1 c. ricotta cheese
1 1/2 c. shredded mozzarella cheese, divided
salt and pepper to taste
1/4 c. Parmesan cheese, grated

Preheat oven to 350°F. Prepare pasta according to package directions; drain. Combine tomato sauce and ricotta cheese. Toss ziti, tomato sauce mixture, 1 cup mozzarella cheese, salt, and pepper to taste. Pour into lightly greased 2-quart casserole. Cover with remaining mozzarella and Parmesan cheese. Bake for 15 to 20 minutes or until thoroughly heated and cheese is melted.

Traditional Lasagne

3 c. ricotta cheese
2 c. shredded mozzarella cheese, divided
3/4 c. Parmesan cheese, grated and divided
1/3 c. fresh parsley, chopped
9 lasagna noodles, cooked and drained
1 30 oz. jar spaghetti sauce

Preheat oven to 350°F. Mix ricotta cheese, 1 cup mozzarella cheese, 1/2 cup Parmesan cheese, and parsley. Spray a 13x9-inch baking dish with nonstick spray. Start layers with 3 lasagna noodles, 1/2 cheese mixture, and 1 cup spaghetti sauce; repeat layer. Top with remaining 3 lasagna noodles, 1 cup spaghetti sauce, 1 cup mozzarella cheese and 1/4 cup Parmesan cheese. Bake for 40 to 45 minutes or until thoroughly heated. Let stand 10 minutes before serving.

Pasta Primavera

1 c. onion, chopped
4 cloves garlic, chopped
4 tbsp. chicken broth, divided
2 15-oz. cans tomato sauce
4 tbsp. honey
2 tsp. dried oregano, crushed
2 tsp. dried basil, crushed
1/2 tsp. white pepper
1 large red pepper, cut in 1-inch strips
1 1/2 c. mushrooms, sliced
1 1/2 c. zucchini, cut into thin sticks
1 1/2 c. carrot, cut into very thin sticks
1 1/2 c. small broccoli florets
3 tbsp. balsamic vinegar, divided
3/4 c. peas
10 oz. pasta, cooked
1/4 c. green onion, chopped
2 tbsp. fresh parsley, chopped

In medium saucepan, cook onion and garlic in 2 tablespoons broth until softened. Add tomato sauce, honey, oregano, basil, and white pepper. Bring to a boil; reduce heat and simmer gently for 20 minutes.

Meanwhile, combine red pepper, mushrooms, zucchini, carrots, broccoli, 2 tablespoons balsamic vinegar, and 2 tablespoons broth in skillet or wok. Stir-fry over high heat until tender-crisp. Add peas and stir-fry an additional 2 minutes; set aside. Add 1 tablespoon balsamic vinegar to sauce and cook for 5 minutes.

Reserve 1 cup sauce to serve with dish. Pour remaining sauce over cooked pasta and toss thoroughly. Add stir-fried vegetables and toss again thoroughly. Sprinkle green onion and parsley over top; serve immediately.

Baked Four-Cheese Ziti

1 lb. ziti, uncooked
1 large jar pasta sauce
1 c. cottage cheese
3/4 c. parsley, chopped
4 oz. Parmesan cheese
8 oz. mozzarella cheese
4 oz. provolone cheese

Preheat oven to 375°F. Cook pasta according to package directions; drain. Coat 13x9x2-inch baking dish with cooking spray. Place a thin layer of sauce in bottom of prepared dish. Continue making layers in this order: pasta, cottage cheese, parsley, sauce, pasta, Parmesan cheese, pasta, mozzarella, parsley, pasta, sauce and parsley. Sprinkle provolone on top. Cover and bake for about 30 minutes or until cheese melts.

Baked Manicotti

8 oz. manicotti, uncooked
15-oz. ricotta cheese, whipped
1/2 c. Parmesan cheese
1 egg, beaten
1/4 c. scallions, sliced
2 tsp. parsley flakes
1/2 tsp. salt
1/2 tsp. pepper
1 large jar spaghetti sauce
grated Parmesan cheese for topping

Preheat oven to 350°F. Prepare pasta according to package directions; drain. In medium bowl blend whipped ricotta, Parmesan cheese, egg, and scallions. Stir in parsley, salt, and pepper. Stuff pasta with cheese mixture. Arrange in a 13x9-inch baking dish. Pour spaghetti sauce evenly over pasta. Sprinkle with additional Parmesan cheese. Cover and bake 35 minutes.

Spaghetti with Meatballs

olive oil

1 large onion, chopped

1 garlic clove, minced

1 bell pepper, chopped

3 bay leaves

2 tbsp. oregano

2 tbsp. basil

2 tbsp. salt

2 tbsp. sugar

2 12-oz. cans tomato paste

4 24-oz. cans tomato purée

2 24-oz. cans whole tomatoes

4 c. water

1 package spaghetti, cooked

Meatballs

1 lb. ground beef

4 cloves garlic

1 tsp. oregano

1 tsp. basil

1 1/2 c. bread crumbs

1 c. Parmesan cheese

vegetable oil

Pour olive oil 1/4 inch deep into a large pot. Lightly brown onion, garlic, and bell pepper in oil. Add all other ingredients except spaghetti; stir well. Add approximately 4 cups water and let simmer at least 5 hours, stirring occasionally. Meanwhile, prepare meatballs by mixing all ingredients together. Fry in a heavy skillet with approximately 1 inch of vegetable oil. Approximately 20 minutes before serving, prepare spaghetti according to package directions. Place meatballs over spaghetti and cover in sauce.

Spaghetti Skillet Dinner

1 lb. spaghetti

1 1/2 lb. ground beef

1 large onion, minced

1 large clove garlic, minced

2 tbsp. vegetable oil

1 28-oz. can tomatoes, crushed

2 tsp. dried oregano

1/4 c. fresh parsley, finely chopped

2 c. cheddar cheese, grated

Prepare pasta according to package directions; drain. Meanwhile, brown beef in large skillet. Drain and set aside.

Preheat oven to 350°F. In skillet, sauté onion and garlic in oil. Return beef to skillet and add tomatoes, oregano, and parsley. Simmer 10 minutes. Add pasta and 1 cup of cheese to simmering tomato mixture; stir. Cover mixture with remaining cheese. Bake for 30 minutes or until top is crispy.

Three Cheese Ditalini

1 lb. Ditalini, uncooked

1 c. milk

3/4 c. ricotta cheese

1/2 c. cheddar cheese, grated

1/3 c. plus 2 tbsp. Parmesan cheese, grated

1/4 c. parsley, chopped

salt and freshly ground black pepper to taste

1/4 c. fine bread crumbs, dry

2 tbsp. margarine, melted

Prepare pasta according to package directions, reducing cooking time by one-third; drain. Preheat oven to 375°F. Meanwhile, combine milk and ricotta in a blender until smooth. Transfer to a medium mixing bowl and stir in cheddar cheese, 1/3 cup Parmesan cheese, parsley, salt and pepper. Stir pasta into cheese mixture until well blended. Pour into a round casserole dish. Combine bread crumbs, margarine, and remaining 2 tablespoons Parmesan cheese in a small bowl until thoroughly mixed. Sprinkle mixture evenly over casserole. Bake about 35 minutes or until bubbling around the edges and bread crumbs are golden brown.

Pasta Vegetable Chowder

1 c. uncooked small shells, elbow macaroni,
  or other small pasta shape
3 c. milk, divided
1 box (10-oz.) frozen mixed vegetables,
  thawed and drained, or 1 1/2 c. chopped fresh
  vegetables (such as zucchini, yellow squash,
  corn, and peas)
1/2 tsp. dried thyme
1/2 tsp. paprika
1 1/2 tbsp. cornstarch
1 can (6-oz.) clams, drained
salt and pepper to taste

Prepare pasta according to package directions;
drain. Rinse pasta under cold water until cool.
Drain again.

Combine 2 1/2 cups milk, vegetables, thyme,
paprika, and pasta in a 2-quart saucepan. Cook
over medium heat until bubbles form around edge
of milk.

In a separate bowl, stir cornstarch and remaining
milk together until cornstarch dissolves. Stir
cornstarch mixture into soup and heat to
simmering. Add clams and simmer, stirring
frequently, for about 3 minutes. Add salt and
pepper to taste. Serve hot.

Chicken Noodle Casserole

8 oz. wide egg noodles, uncooked
1/2 c. nonfat sour cream
1 c. low-sodium chicken broth
4 tbsp. grated Parmesan cheese, divided
1/2 c. egg substitute
2 tbsp. Dijon mustard
1 1/2 c. chopped broccoli, blanched and drained
1 1/2 c. skinless and boneless chicken breast
  meat, cooked
2 tbsp. bread crumbs

Prepare egg noodles according to package
directions; drain.

Heat oven to 350° F. Whisk sour cream, chicken
broth, 2 tablespoons Parmesan cheese, egg
substitute, and mustard in a bowl until blended.
Add noodles, broccoli, and chicken; toss well.
Transfer mixture to a 9x12-inch baking dish.

Combine remaining cheese and bread crumbs in a
small bowl and sprinkle over casserole. Bake
uncovered until bubbling around edges and top is
golden brown, about 35 minutes. Let stand 5
minutes before serving.

Fettuccine With Light Alfredo Sauce

1 lb. fettucine, linguine or spaghetti, uncooked
1 c. evaporated skim milk
1/2 c. grated Parmesan cheese
4 oz. green onions, sliced (white parts only)
1/2 c. chopped fresh parsley
white pepper to taste

Prepare pasta according to package directions;
drain. In a large saucepan, bring evaporated milk
to a simmer over moderate heat. Stir in Parmesan,
green onions, and parsley.

As soon as cheese has melted and sauce is thick
and creamy, pour over cooked pasta. Season to
taste with white pepper.

Ziti With Mixed Vegetables

8 oz. uncooked ziti
1 1/2 tbsp. vegetable oil
2 scallions, finely chopped
1/2 tsp. Italian seasoning
2 tbsp. horseradish sauce
1/2 c. skim milk
4 oz. (1 c.) grated cheddar cheese
1 1/2 c. mixed vegetables, cooked
salt and fresh ground black pepper to taste

Prepare pasta according to package directions. Meanwhile, heat oil in a medium saucepan. Add scallions and sauté over medium heat until limp. Do not brown.

Remove from heat. Stir in Italian seasoning, horseradish sauce, milk, and cheese. Cook over medium heat until thickened. Stir in cooked vegetables and heat.

Place pasta in a large, heated bowl, and toss with sauce.

Pizza Pasta Salad

1 lb. uncooked Rotini, twists or spirals
3 oz. pepperoni, sliced (about 3/4 c.)
4 oz. sliced provolone cheese (about 1 c.)
12 cherry tomatoes, halved (about 1 1/2 c.)
1/2 c. grated Parmesan cheese
1/2 c. non-fat Italian salad dressing
1 tsp. Italian seasoning
1/2 tsp. garlic, minced
2 1/2 rounds (about 7 inches ea.) of pita bread
1 green bell pepper, ribs and seeds removed, sliced into rings

Prepare pasta according to package directions. While pasta is cooking, cut pepperoni slices into fourths and slice Provolone cheese into matchstick-sized pieces. Place in a large bowl. Add cherry tomatoes, Parmesan cheese, Italian dressing, Italian seasoning, and garlic.

When pasta is done, drain and rinse with cold water. Drain again. Add pasta to cheese mixture and mix well. Quarter pita bread rounds and place around a large platter. Top with pasta salad and garnish with green pepper rings.

Spaghetti With Clam Sauce

1 lb. uncooked spaghetti or linguine
2 tbsp. vegetable oil
2 cloves garlic, minced
2 cans (6 1/2-oz. ea.) chopped clams, drained (reserve liquid)
1/2 c. fresh parsley, chopped
1/4 c. dry white wine
1 tsp. basil leaves
1/4 tsp. white pepper

Cook pasta according to package directions; drain.

In a medium skillet, heat oil. Add garlic. Stir in reserved clam liquid and parsley; cook and stir 3 minutes. Add clams, wine, basil and pepper. Simmer on low heat for 5 minutes. Pour sauce over spaghetti and serve immediately.

Linguine With Scallops

1 lb. uncooked linguine
1 green bell pepper, ribs and seeds removed, diced
1 medium onion, cut in half and sliced thin
2 cloves garlic, minced
1 tsp. olive or vegetable oil
1 28-oz. can diced tomatoes or tomato wedges, drained
1/4 c. pitted and chopped black olives
1 tbsp. fresh oregano, chopped (1 tsp. dried oregano)
1 lb. small scallops
1/4 c. fresh parsley, chopped
coarsely ground black pepper

Prepare pasta according to package directions. While pasta is cooking, sauté green pepper, onion, and garlic in oil in a large skillet over medium heat for 5 minutes or until edges of onion turn golden. Add tomatoes, olives, and oregano; heat until simmering. Add scallops and simmer 3 to 4 minutes.

When pasta is done, drain well. Toss pasta with sauce. Add parsley. Sprinkle with pepper and serve immediately.

Salmon-Stuffed Pasta Shells With Dill Sauce

24 large uncooked pasta shells
2 eggs, beaten
2 c. part-skim ricotta cheese
1/4 c. onion, chopped
1 red bell pepper, ribs and seeds removed, diced
1/4 c. parsley, snipped
1/2 tsp. lemon peel, grated fine
1 can salmon, drained and flaked
1 tsp. seafood seasoning
1 c. evaporated skim milk
Dill Sauce (recipe follows)

Cook pasta according to package directions; drain well. Cool on waxed paper or aluminum foil to keep shells from sticking together.

Combine eggs, ricotta cheese, onion, bell pepper, parsley, lemon peel, salmon, and seafood seasoning. Pour evaporated skim milk into lightly oiled 9x12x2-inch baking dish.

Fill each pasta shell with a heaping tablespoon of filling. Arrange shells in casserole; cover with aluminum foil. Bake at 350° F for 30 to 35 minutes or until hot and bubbly. Remove casserole from oven; arrange shells on serving platter. Serve with dill sauce.

Dill Sauce

1 1/2 tbsp. butter
1 1/2 tbsp. all-purpose flour
1/4 tsp. salt
1/8 tsp. pepper
1 1/2 c. skim milk
3 tbsp. fine-snipped fresh dill or 2 tsp. dried dill weed
1 tbsp. lemon juice

Melt butter in small saucepan over medium heat; stir in flour, salt, and pepper. Remove saucepan from heat; gradually add skim milk, stirring until mixture is smooth.

Return to medium heat; bring to boiling, stirring constantly. Reduce heat, simmer 1 minute. Remove from heat; stir in dill and lemon juice.

Rice Dishes

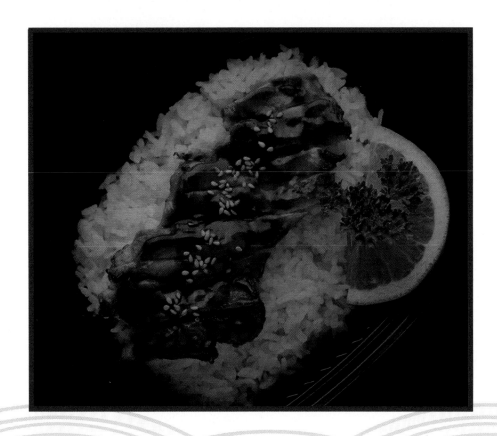

Purée:
To convert a food into a liquid or heavy paste
with a blender or food processor.

Garnish:
o decorate food with colorful pieces, such as parsley.

Bacon Cheddar Rice

3 c. water
1/2 tsp. salt
3 c. quick-cooking rice
1 c. cheddar cheese, shredded
1 c. sour cream
6 slices bacon, cooked and crumbled
2 scallions, thinly sliced

Bring water and salt to boil in medium saucepan. Stir in rice and cover. Remove from heat and let stand 5 minutes. Stir in remaining ingredients and serve.

Chicken and Rice Casserole

1 c. plain rice
1 c. cold milk
1/2 tsp. salt
1 can cream of chicken soup
1 can cream of mushroom soup
1 can cream of broccoli soup
1 stick butter
6 boneless and skinless chicken breasts
dash of paprika

Preheat oven to 300°F. Spread uncooked rice in a 9x13-inch baking dish. Mix milk and salt together and pour over rice. In large saucepan, mix soups and butter. Simmer until heated through and butter is melted, stirring constantly. Pour soup mixture over rice. Place chicken breasts on top of rice. Sprinkle with paprika and bake for two hours.

Stuffed Bell Peppers

6 medium bell peppers, topped and seeded
1 lb. ground beef
1/3 c. onion, chopped
1/2 tsp. salt
1/2 tsp. black pepper
1 16-oz. can tomatoes
1/2 c. water
1/2 c. long-grain rice, uncooked
1 tsp. Worcestershire sauce
1 c. shredded cheese (American or
   mild cheddar)

Preheat oven to 350°F. Meanwhile, bring a pot of salted water to boil. Put peppers in water and cook for about five minutes; drain. Sprinkle inside of peppers with salt; set aside. Cook ground beef and onion in a heavy skillet until brown; drain. Season with salt and pepper. Stir in tomatoes, water, rice, and Worcestershire sauce. Cover and simmer until rice is tender. Stir in cheese; stuff peppers with mixture. Bake uncovered for 20-25 minutes.

Quick Chicken and Rice Cacciatore

4 boneless and skinless chicken breast
   halves, cubed
1/2 c. chopped onion
2 tbsp. vegetable oil
1 green pepper, chopped
1/2 tsp. dried whole oregano
1/2 tsp. dried whole basil
1 16 oz. jar spaghetti sauce
1 1/4 c. water
1 1/2 c. instant rice, uncooked
1 8-oz. can whole water chestnuts, drained
   and diced

Sauté chicken and chopped onion in oil in a large skillet until lightly browned, stirring often. Add green pepper, oregano, basil, spaghetti sauce, and water. Bring mixture to a boil and mix thoroughly. Add rice and water chestnuts. Cover and remove from heat. Let stand 5 to 10 minutes or until liquid is absorbed and rice is tender.

Rice Casserole

3/4 stick butter
1 can onion soup
1/2 soup can water
1 c. mushrooms
1/2 c. rice, uncooked
1 can water chestnuts, sliced

Preheat oven to 325°F. Melt butter in casserole dish. Stir in mushrooms and water chestnuts. Remove from heat. Add remaining ingredients and stir slightly. Cover and bake 1 1/2 hours.

Sweet and Sour Chicken

4 chicken breast halves
1/2 c. white vinegar
3 tbsp. brown sugar
1 tbsp. soy sauce
1 20-oz. can crushed pineapple with juice
1/2 tsp. pepper
4 c. rice, cooked

Preheat oven to 250°F. Place chicken in baking dish. Mix vinegar, brown sugar, soy sauce, pineapple, and pepper in a saucepan and heat until boiling. Pour mixture over chicken and bake for 2 1/2 to 3 hours. Serve over cooked rice.

Poppa John's Red Rice

2 c. uncooked long-grain rice
6 slices bacon
2 medium finely chopped onions
1 8-oz. can tomato sauce
1 6-oz. can tomato paste
1 tbsp. sugar
2 tsp. Worcestershire sauce
dash of hot sauce

Preheat oven to 325°F. Cook rice according to package directions; set aside.

Meanwhile, fry bacon in a medium skillet until crisp. Remove bacon and reserve 1/4 cup drippings in skillet. Crumble bacon and set aside.

Cook onions in drippings over medium-high heat, stirring constantly, until tender. Add tomato sauce, tomato paste, sugar, Worcestershire sauce, and hot sauce. Bring to a boil; reduce heat. Simmer, uncovered, for 10 minutes. Stir in rice. Place rice mixture in a buttered 2-quart casserole. Bake for 45 minutes or until liquid is absorbed and rice is tender. Sprinkle with bacon. Serve immediately.

Beef Stroganoff

1 lb. round steak, cut into thin strips
1/2 c. onion, chopped
2 tbsp. butter
1 garlic clove
1 can cream of mushroom soup
1/4 c. water
1/2 c. sour cream
1/2 tsp. paprika
1 c. rice, cooked
salt and pepper to taste

Melt butter in large skillet. Sauté steak, onion, and garlic until steak is just browned. Remove garlic and stir in all remaining ingredients except rice. Cover. Cook over low heat, about 45 minutes or until steak is tender. Serve over rice.

Quick Sausage Casserole

1 lb. sausage
1 c. rice, uncooked
2 cans chicken noodle soup
1/4 c. onion, chopped
1/4 c. green pepper, chopped
1 c. celery, chopped
2 1/2 c. water
1 1/2 tsp. soy sauce
1/2 tsp. salt

Preheat oven to 350°F. Brown sausage in a heavy skillet; drain. Mix all remaining ingredients and place in an oven-safe baking dish, tossing in browned sausage. Bake for 30 minutes and serve.

Ham and Broccoli Casserole

1 6-oz. pkg. instant rice
1 can mushroom soup
1 c. mayonnaise
1 c. mushrooms, sliced
1 tsp. curry powder
1 1/2 tsp. dry mustard
1 tsp. paprika
10-oz. package frozen broccoli, chopped
  and thawed
3/4 lb. diced ham
1 c. sharp cheddar cheese

Preheat oven to 350°F. Cook rice until tender. Mix soup, mayonnaise, mushrooms, and spices in a large bowl. Layer rice, soup mixture, ham, and broccoli in a casserole dish. Sprinkle top with cheddar cheese and paprika. Bake 45 minutes or until bubbly.

Hamburger Squash Surprise

1 1/2 lb. yellow squash, chopped
2 tbsp. butter
2 c. instant rice
1 lb. ground beef
1 large onion, chopped
1 15-oz. can tomato sauce
1/4 tsp. garlic powder
salt and pepper to taste

Boil chopped squash in water until tender. Drain well and add butter. Prepare rice according to package directions. Meanwhile, brown ground beef and onion in a heavy skillet; drain. Combine squash, ground beef mixture, and tomato sauce in skillet. Add garlic, salt, and pepper. Simmer for 15 minutes. Mix in rice and serve.

Shrimp and Pepper Rice

1 red bell pepper, diced
1 yellow bell pepper, diced
2 large cloves garlic, minced
5 tbsp. olive oil, divided
1 28-oz. jar pasta sauce
3 cans chicken broth
1 1/2 c. rice
1 lb. large shrimp, peeled and deveined
1/3 c. Parmesan cheese, grated

In large skillet, sauté red and yellow peppers and garlic in 3 tablespoons olive oil; set aside. In large saucepan, combine pasta sauce with chicken broth; heat thoroughly. In large stockpot, lightly sauté rice in remaining olive oil. Add 1 cup heated pasta sauce mixture to rice. Cook over low to medium heat, stirring frequently.

Continue to gradually add heated pasta sauce mixture. Stir and cook about 30 to 40 minutes or until rice is tender. With about 10 minutes left for rice to cook, add shrimp to skillet with peppers and garlic; sauté until shrimp just turn pink. Stir Parmesan cheese into rice. Spoon hot rice into a large serving bowl and top with shrimp and peppers.

Lemon Rice

1 medium onion, chopped
2 cloves garlic, minced
1 tbsp. vegetable oil
2 c. long-grain rice, uncooked
4 chicken bouillon cubes
4 c. water
3 tbsp. lemon juice
1/2 c. parsley, chopped

In a small skillet, sauté onion and garlic in oil until tender. Stir in all remaining ingredients except parsley; bring to a boil. Cover and reduce heat. Simmer until rice is tender and liquid is absorbed, about 20 minutes. Stir in parsley and serve.

Southern Hash

1 lb. ground beef
1 onion, chopped
1 green pepper, chopped
2 c. canned tomatoes
1 c. rice, cooked
1 c. cheddar cheese, grated

In a heavy skillet, brown ground beef; drain. Return to pan and add onion, pepper, and tomatoes. Let cook about 3 minutes. Add rice and pour into a 1 1/2-quart covered casserole dish. Bake for 45 minutes. Remove from oven and top with cheddar cheese. Return to oven until cheese is melted, about 10 minutes.

Baked Mushrooms and Rice

1 small can mushrooms
4 green onions, sliced
1 stick butter
1 c. rice, uncooked
1 tsp. oregano
2 cans beef broth
1/2 c. water

Preheat oven to 425°F. Sauté mushrooms and onions in butter in a small skillet. Mix remaining ingredients with sautéed vegetables and place in 2-quart casserole dish. Cover and bake for 45 minutes.

Spicy Chicken Rice Bake

1 c. long-grain rice
1/2 lb. Monterey Jack cheese
1 tsp. salt
2 c. sour cream
1 c. green chilies, chopped
1/2 c. sharp cheddar cheese, grated
Dash of paprika

Preheat oven to 350°F. Meanwhile, prepare rice according to package directions. Melt Monterey Jack cheese in hot rice. Stir in remaining ingredients except cheddar cheese and paprika. Pour into a greased 1 1/2-quart casserole dish. Top with cheddar cheese and paprika. Bake for 30 minutes.

Sour Cream Rice

1 c. rice, cooked and divided
1 pt. sour cream, divided
1 tbsp. sugar, divided
1 lb. cheddar cheese, shredded and divided
red pepper, crushed
salt to taste

Preheat oven to 350°F. Place 1/2 cup rice in casserole. Layer with 1/2 pint sour cream, 1/2 tablespoon sugar, and 1/2 pound cheese; sprinkle with crushed red pepper and salt. Repeat layer. Bake for 30 minutes.

Chorizo and Rice Wrapped In Cabbage Leaves

1/3 c. rice (not converted)
1 c. water
1/4 tsp. salt
1/4 lb. dry chorizo or pepperoni
1 medium cucumber
1 bunch green onions
4 large cabbage leaves
3 tbsp. olive oil
1 tbsp. parsley, minced
1 tsp. garlic, minced
1/4 tsp. hot red pepper sauce
salt to taste

In saucepan, combine rice, water, and salt. Bring to boil; cover and simmer 30 minutes. Turn off heat and let sit 10 minutes. Uncover and cool slightly. (Rice will be sticky.)

Cut chorizo and cucumber into long, 1/4-inch wide by 6-inch long matchsticks. Cut green onions into 6-inch lengths. Bring large pot of water to boil; add cabbage leaves. Cook 30 seconds or until leaves are softened; rinse in cold water and drain on paper towels. Trim each cabbage leaf to a 5x6-inch rectangle.

Spoon 1/4 cup rice along 6-inch length of each cabbage leaf, not far from edge. Arrange 4 rows of chorizo sticks (using extra pieces, if necessary, to make them 6 inches long), 2 green onion pieces, and 1 cucumber stick over rice, and gently press into rice. Roll up cabbage leaf tightly, brushing ends with oil to seal. Gently squeeze roll so that filling holds together. Cut each roll into 1-inch pieces. Arrange pieces cut-side down on serving dish. In small bowl, combine oil, parsley, garlic, pepper sauce, and salt to taste. Spoon over chorizo rolls and serve at room temperature.

Rice Stuffed Mushrooms

3 tbsp. onion, minced
1 tbsp. butter
24 large, fresh mushrooms, stems removed, washed, and dried
1 tsp. salt
1 tbsp. chili sauce
1 c. extra long grain rice, cooked
1/4 tsp. ground black pepper
1 tbsp. lemon juice
1/2 c. nut meats, chopped fine
1/4 c. melted butter

In small skillet, cook onion in 1 tablespoon butter until tender but not brown. Add all remaining ingredients except melted butter. Press rice mixture into each mushroom cavity. Place mushroom caps on rack in broiler. Drizzle with melted butter and broil until golden brown. Makes 24 mushrooms.

Rice and Noodle Casserole

1/2 lb. butter
1/2 lb. very fine noodles
2 c. instant rice
2 cans (10 3/4 oz.) onion soup
2 cans (10 3/4 oz.) chicken broth
1 tsp. soy sauce
1 c. water
8 oz. canned sliced water chestnuts, drained

Melt butter in a large kettle. Add noodles and cook until lightly browned, stirring frequently. Add remaining ingredients and mix well. Pour mixture into 3-quart casserole. Bake at 350° F for 45 minutes.

Quick Broccoli and Rice Casserole

1 pkg. (10 oz.) frozen broccoli and cheese sauce
1 c. chicken, ham, or turkey, cooked and cubed
1/2 c. quick-cooking rice
1/2 c. whole milk
2 tbsp. Parmesan cheese, grated

NOTE: Cooking times are based on the use of a 625-750 watt microwave oven and food quantities for 2 servings. Adjust cooking times as required.

Cook broccoli and cheese sauce according to package directions. Turn into a 1-quart casserole. Add cooked meat, rice, milk and cheese; blend thoroughly. Cover and microwave on high until rice is tender (about 6 minutes), stirring once. Serve.

Wild Herbed Rice

1/4 c. butter
1 c. brown rice
1 c. wild rice
1 c. onion, chopped
1 c. celery , chopped
1 lb. fresh mushrooms, sliced
3 3/4 c. chicken broth
1/4 c. fresh parsley, chopped
1/2 tsp. salt
1/4 tsp. dried thyme
fresh ground black pepper
1/4 c. pecans, chopped (optional)

In a large saucepan, melt butter over medium heat. Add brown rice, wild rice, onion, and celery; sauté for approximately 5 minutes or until onion and celery are tender. Add mushrooms, chicken broth, parsley, salt, thyme, and pepper. (Add pecans if desired.) Bring to a boil; reduce heat to low and simmer for 1 hour or until liquid has evaporated.

Down-Home Fried Rice

3 tbsp. canola oil
1 1/2 c. onion, cut in half and slivered
4 ribs celery, washed and sliced diagonally
    into 1/4-inch thick pieces
2 cloves garlic, minced fine
1 tbsp. ginger, minced fine
small red bell pepper, cored, seeded,
    and diced into 1/4-inch pieces
4 c. long-grain rice, cooked
1/4 c. no-sodium beef broth, defatted
1/8 lb. cured ham, sliced thin and shredded
1 lb. shrimp, peeled, deveined, cooked,
    and cut in half crosswise
1/4 lb. snow peas, lightly blanched and
    cut lengthwise into thin strips
2 eggs
2 tbsp. soy sauce
1/2 c. scallions, cleaned and sliced thin

Heat canola oil in large, heavy casserole over medium-low heat. Add onion, celery, garlic, and ginger and cook, stirring constantly, for 5 minutes.

Add red pepper; cook 3 minutes. Add rice, broth, and ham; cook 2 minutes, stirring ingredients to mix. Add shrimp and snow peas. Cook 1 minute longer. Remove from heat.

In bowl, beat eggs and soy sauce together. Push rice to sides of casserole, making a well in center. Return casserole to medium-low heat; pour egg mixture into well.

Stir with fork for about 1 minute until eggs are just set. Gently fold into rice. Heat through and stir in scallions. Serve immediately.

Orange Rice

3 tbsp. butter
2/3 c. celery, diced, with leaves
2 tbsp. onion, chopped
1 1/2 c. water
1 c. fresh orange juice
grated rind of 1 orange
1 1/4 tsp. salt
1/4 tsp. thyme
1 c. rice

Melt butter in a heavy saucepan. Add celery and onion; cook until onion is soft and golden. Add water, orange juice, rind, salt and thyme. Bring to a boil. Add rice slowly, stirring constantly. Cover; reduce heat and simmer for 25 minutes or until rice is tender.

Fiesta Rice

1 medium onion, chopped fine
1/2 small green pepper, chopped
3 tbsp. butter
16 oz. stewed tomatoes
1 tsp. salt
1/8 tsp. pepper
3 c. rice, cooked

Cook and stir onion and green pepper in butter in 10-inch skillet until onion is tender. Stir in tomatoes, salt, pepper and rice. Simmer, uncovered, over low heat about 15 minutes or to desired consistency.

Hot German Rice Salad

6 slices bacon, cut into 1/4-inch pieces
1 medium onion, chopped fine
1/2 c. cider vinegar
3 tbsp. sugar
2 tbsp. water
1/2 tsp. salt
1/4 tsp. black pepper

1 small carrot, grated
2 tbsp. fresh parsley, chopped
4 c. cooked rice

In a large skillet, cook bacon until crisp. Pour off all but 2 tablespoons fat. Add onion, vinegar, sugar, water, salt, and pepper. Cook until onion is tender. Stir in rice, carrot, and parsley. Continue cooking until heated through, about 5 minutes.

Spanish Rice With Avocado

1 tbsp. butter
1 tbsp. olive oil
1 small onion, chopped fine
1 clove garlic, minced fine
1 c. rice
1/4 tsp. salt
1/4 tsp. dried oregano, crushed
1/4 tsp. ground cumin
1/4 tsp. ground tumeric
1 can (14 1/2 oz.) chicken broth
1 small avocado

Place butter and oil in a 2-quart pan over medium heat. When butter is melted, add onion and garlic; cook until onion is tender. Add rice and cook, stirring constantly, 3 minutes or until rice looks milky and opaque.

Add salt, oregano, cumin, tumeric, and chicken broth. Bring to a boil. Cover; reduce heat and simmer for 20-25 minutes or until rice is tender and all liquid is absorbed.

Peel and pit avocado; dice. Fluff rice with fork; add avocado and toss gently. Turn off heat; let stand 5 minutes before serving.

Mexican Rice

1 c. rice
2 c. water
1/4 tsp. salt
2/3 c. Monterey Jack cheese, grated
1 1/4 c. plain yogurt
1 green pepper, chopped
1/3 c. cheddar cheese, grated
1/2 c. corn, cooked (optional)
1/4 c. black olives, chopped (optional)

Bring water and salt to a boil in a saucepan; add rice. Cover and cook over low heat until done (about 25 minutes). Transfer cooked rice to a serving bowl; mix in vegetables, Monterey Jack cheese, and yogurt. Stir in cheddar cheese and cover, allowing cheese to melt.

Pecan and Wild-Rice Pilaf

4 c. chicken broth
1 c. wild rice, rinsed well
1 3/4 c. wheat pilaf
1 c. pecan halves
1 c. currants, dried
1 bunch scallions, sliced thin
1/2 c. Italian parsley, chopped
1/2 c. fresh mint leaves, chopped
zest of 2 oranges, grated
2 tsp. olive oil
1 tsp. orange juice
fresh ground black pepper

In a medium saucepan, bring broth to a boil. Add wild rice and return to a boil. Reduce heat to medium-low. Cover and cook for 50 minutes or until rice is tender. Do not overcook. Remove to a large bowl.

While rice is cooking, bring 2 1/4 cups water to a boil in another saucepan. Stir in pilaf; cover and return to a boil. Reduce heat to low and simmer 15 minutes or until pilaf is tender.

Remove from heat, let sit 15 minutes, then add to wild rice. Add remaining ingredients and toss well. Serve at room temperature.

Curried Rice

1 onion, chopped
1 green pepper, chopped
2 tbsp. butter
1 tsp. curry powder
1 egg yolk, slightly beaten
3 c. rice, cooked
1/4 tsp. salt
1/4 tsp. pepper
1/4 tsp. cayenne

Sauté onion and green pepper in butter until onion is tender. Stir in curry powder, egg, salt, pepper, and cayenne. Mix into hot rice. Sprinkle with chopped olive if available.

Southern-Style Honey Rice

4 c. rice, cooked
1/2 c. roasted peanuts, chopped
1/4 c. butter
1/4 c. honey
1 tsp. cinnamon
3/4 tsp. ginger
chopped parsley

Combine rice and peanuts. Set aside and keep warm. Combine butter and honey in a saucepan, cook over low heat just until butter melts. Stir in cinnamon and ginger. Pour over rice, stirring well. Garnish with parsley.

Rice With Peas

2 tbsp. vegetable oil
1/2 tsp. black mustard seeds
2 c. basmati rice
1 c. fresh peas *or* 1 c. frozen peas
3 c. water
1 tsp. salt

Heat oil in pot. Add mustard seeds and leave them for 10-20 seconds. Add rice and *fresh* peas and stir-fry for 1 minute. Add water and salt. Cover and bring to a boil. Reduce heat to very low and cook until rice is almost done, about 15-25 minutes.

If using frozen peas, thaw them under running hot water. Add to rice about 5 minutes before the cooking process is finished.

Red Beans

1 lb. salt pork
1 lb. red kidney beans
1 bell pepper, seeded and chopped
1 onion, chopped
1 stalk celery
2 cloves garlic
1 tsp. Italian seasoning
1 hot pepper

Boil pork for 5 minutes to get rid of salt. Transfer pork to another pan of hot water and add beans; water should be one-half inch above beans. Immediately add bell pepper, onion, celery, garlic, Italian seasoning and whole hot pepper. Cook slowly, two to three hours, until gravy is thick and beans tender. Just before serving, add another pinch of Italian seasoning. Salt to taste. Serve with rice.

Dirty Rice

2 tsp. chicken fat
1/2 lb. chicken gizzards, ground
1/4 lb. ground pork
1 bay leaf
1 yellow onion, minced
1 1/2 stalks celery, minced
1/2 green bell pepper, minced
1 clove garlic, minced
1 tsp. hot red pepper sauce
1 tsp. salt
1 tsp. black pepper
2 tsp. paprika
1 tsp. dry mustard
1 tsp. cumin
1/2 tsp. thyme
1/2 tsp. oregano
2 tsp. butter
2 c. pork stock
1/2 lb. chicken livers, ground
1 c. rice

Place fat, gizzards, pork, and bay leaf in large, heavy skillet over high heat; cook until meat is thoroughly browned, about 6 minutes, stirring occasionally. Stir in onion, celery, bell pepper, garlic, pepper sauce, salt, pepper, paprika, mustard, cumin, thyme, and oregano; stir thoroughly, scraping bottom of pan. Add butter and stir until melted. Reduce heat to medium and cook about 8 minutes, stirring constantly and scraping bottom of pan. Add stock and stir until any mixture sticking to pan bottom comes loose; cook about 8 minutes over high heat, stirring once. Stir in chicken livers and cook about 2 minutes. Add rice and stir thoroughly; cover pan and reduce heat to very low; cook about 5 minutes. Remove from heat and leave covered until rice is tender, about 10 minutes. Remove bay leaf and serve immediately.

Wild Rice Amandine Casserole

2 tbsp. onion, chopped
2 tbsp. fresh chives, chopped fine
1 tsp. shallot, chopped fine
3 tbsp. green bell pepper, chopped fine
1/4 c. olive oil
2 c. wild rice, rinsed well and drained
4 1/2 c. chicken broth, heated
salt and pepper to taste
3/4 c. blanched almonds, slivered

In a large saucepan, cook onion, chives, shallot, and pepper in oil over medium-low heat, stirring occasionally, until vegetables are softened. Add rice and cook, stirring constantly, for 1 minute. Stir in broth, season with salt and pepper to taste, and add almonds.

Transfer mixture to a 4-quart casserole. Cover and bake at 325°F for 35 minutes; remove and stir. Replace and continue cooking until rice is tender about 40 minutes more.

Shrimp Fried Rice Shanghai

1/4 lb. shrimp, shelled and deveined
1 tsp. cornstarch
2 tsp. water
1/4 tsp. salt
5 tbsp. oil
3 eggs, beaten
1/4 tsp. salt
3 1/2 c. rice, cooked and allowed to cool
1/2 tsp. salt
2 scallions, chopped fine

If shrimp are large, cut crosswise into 1/2-inch pieces. Dissolve cornstarch in water and add salt to make coating. Mix with shrimp and set aside. Heat wok over high heat until hot. Add 2 tablespoons oil, coat, and heat for a few seconds. Reduce heat to medium, add shrimp, and stir-fry briskly for 1-2 minutes until shrimp are pink and firm. Pour into dish and set aside.

Clean wok and heat over high heat. Beat eggs with salt. Add remaining oil to pan, coat, and heat until very hot. Pour in eggs. As eggs puff around edges, push mass with spatula to far end of pan, tilting pan back so that runny eggs slide onto hot surface. Continue this process until eggs are soft and fluffy. Scrape cooked eggs into a dish.

Set pan over medium heat. Add rice and stir-fry about 1 minute. Add salt to taste. Add scallions and stir briefly. Add shrimp and eggs and stir rapidly, turning and folding, for about 1 minute. Eggs should be in small pieces and well mixed with rice and shrimp. Pour into hot serving dish.

Country Rice

1/3 c. chicken stock made without salt or fat
1/3 c. green onion, chopped
pinch fresh ground black pepper
1/3 c. white rice

Bring stock to a boil with green onion and pepper. Add rice. Reduce heat and simmer for 20 minutes.

Peppery Rice

2 c. brown rice
4 c. chicken broth
1/4 c. green onion, chopped
1/4 c. red peppers, chopped
1/2 tsp. salt
1/4 tsp. garlic powder
1/4 tsp. cayenne pepper
1/4 tsp. white pepper

Place rice and chicken broth in a 3-quart saucepan. Bring to a boil. Reduce heat, cover, and simmer for 20 minutes. Add remaining ingredients and simmer another 20 minutes.

Index

Pasta With Meat 5
Bacon and Cream Cheese Pasta 6
Beef 'n Macaroni 7
Cheeseburger Macaroni 6
Chorizo Noodle Casserole 8
Creamy Ham Rotini Bake 6
Easy Pasta 6
Fettuccine With Peas and Ham 8
Ham and Asparagus Pasta 8
Inside-Out Calzone 7
Italian Sausage Fettucine 9
Pasta and Pork Stir-Fry 7
Pasta With Tomatoes, White Beans,
    and Pepperoni 9
Pierogi With Meat 10
Polish Reuben Casserole 9
Quick Baked Pasta 10
Rigatoni With Sausage 10
Sausage Lasagna Rolls 6
Sausage Spaghetti 7
Swiss Spaghetti 10

Pasta With Seafood 11
Angel Hair Pasta With Shrimp 16
Fettuccine With Vegetables
    and Scallops 14
Garlic Shrimp and Pasta 12
Lemon Scallop Spaghetti 13
Linguine Tuna Salad 12
Mostaccioli and Shrimp With
    Tangerine-Basil Sauce 15
Rotini With Tuna and Tomato 15
Salmon and Spinach Noodle Bake .. 14
Seafood Pasta Salad 12
Shellfish Shell Marinara 16
Shrimp and Chicken Spaghetti 13
Shrimp and Crab Spaghetti 15
Shrimp with Tomato Cream Pasta ... 13
Tuna Pasta Salad 12

Pasta With Chicken 17
Baked Chicken and Pasta
    Casserole 19
Bow Ties With Asian Chicken 22
Chicken and Broccoli Pasta Dijon ... 20
Chicken and Red Pesto Linguine 22
Chicken Lasagne 20
Chicken Mushroom Fettuccine 21
Chicken Noodle Casserole 21
Chicken Spaghetti 18
Citrus Chicken Pasta 18
Easy Chicken Fettuccine 18
Garlic Pasta Chicken Salad 18
Quick Chicken Casserole 21
Quick Chicken Parmesan 19
Spaghetti with Chicken Sauce 19

Pasta With Vegetables 23
Acorn Squash 'n Pasta Soup 29
Country Fettuccine 25
Eggplant Lasagne 27
Eggplant Parmesan 26
Fast Primavera 28
Fettuccine with Spinach Sauce 26
Fresh Tomato and Basil Pasta 26
Green and White Lasagne 30

Lemon Pasta with Roasted
    Asparagus 27
Mostaccioli with Spinach 25
Pasta With Roasted Vegetables 30
Pasta with Spicy Cucumber Sauce .. 24
Penne With Zucchini
    And Parmesan 30
Primavera With Zucchini, Tomato,
    and Corn 29
Quick-Baked Creamy Pasta 24
Spinach and Bacon Bowtie Pasta 24
Spinach Lasagne 25
Three Bean Pasta 29
Tomato and Basil Pasta 24
Vegetable Lasagne 28

Pasta Salads 31
Bistro Chicken Pasta Salad 32
Blue Cheese Pasta Salad 33
Chicken Pasta Salad 32
Creamy Pesto Pasta Salad 32
Double-Decker Pasta Salad 34
Dressed-Up Pasta and
    Pepper Salad 33
Macaroni Salad 32
Orange Pasta Salad with
    Light Orange Vinaigrette 34
Pasta and Beef Salad 34
Pasta and Walnut Fruit Salad 35
Radiatore Salad With Salmon
    and Papaya 35
Ravioli Salad 33
Rigatoni-Turkey Salad 35
Shell Salad 33
Shrimp and Feta Cheese Salad 36
Springtime Pasta Salad 36
Tangy Pasta Salad 32

Ethnic Dishes 37
Asian Chicken Pasta 40
Asian Chicken Pasta Salad 44
Cheesy Tex-Mex Chili-Mac 39
Chinese Noodle Salad 41
Chinese Pasta Salad 43
Chinese Pasta Salad with Tuna 38
Irish Lasagne 42
Italian Pasta Salad 38
Italian Soup 39
Japanese Orange Fettuccine 42
Japanese Pasta 42
Mandarin Chicken Pasta 38
Mediterranean Fettuccine
    With Shrimp and Spinach 44
Mexicali Beef Salsa Macaroni 38
Mexican Pasta Casserole 40
Mexican Pasta Pie 44
Oriental Pepper Steak 39
Pasta Chili 41
Pasta With Chinese Tahini Sauce 43
Quick and Easy Chop Suey 38
Spanish Rice 40

Pasta Classics 45
Baked Four-Cheese Ziti 48
Baked Manicotti 48
Chicken Noodle Casserole 50

Classic Baked Mostaccioli 47
Easy Lasagne 46
Easy Macaroni 'n Cheese 47
Feta Fettuccine 47
Fettuccine With Light
    Alfredo Sauce 50
Lasagna Casserole 46
Linguine With Scallops 52
Pasta Primavera 48
Pasta Vegetable Chowder 50
Pizza Pasta Salad 51
Quick Baked Ziti 47
Salmon-Stuffed Pasta Shells
    With Dill Sauce 52
Spaghetti Skillet Dinner 49
Spaghetti With Clam Sauce 51
Spaghetti with Meatballs 49
Spicy Macaroni 'n Cheese 46
Tasty Spaghetti in White Sauce 46
Three Cheese Ditalini 49
Traditional Lasagne 47
Ziti With Mixed Vegetables 51

Rice Dishes 53
Bacon Cheddar Rice 54
Baked Mushrooms and Rice 57
Beef Stroganoff 55
Chicken and Rice Casserole 54
Chorizo and Rice Wrapped
    In Cabbage Leaves 58
Country Rice 63
Curried Rice 61
Dirty Rice 62
Down-Home Fried Rice 59
Fiesta Rice 60
Ham and Broccoli Casserole 56
Hamburger Squash Surprise 56
Hot German Rice Salad 60
Lemon Rice 57
Mexican Rice 61
Orange Rice 60
Pecan and Wild-Rice Pilaf 61
Peppery Rice 63
Poppa John's Red Rice 55
Quick Broccoli and
    Rice Casserole 59
Quick Chicken and
    Rice Cacciatore 54
Quick Sausage Casserole 56
Red Beans 62
Rice and Noodle Casserole 58
Rice Casserole 55
Rice Stuffed Mushrooms 58
Rice With Peas 62
Shrimp and Pepper Rice 56
Shrimp Fried Rice Shanghai 63
Sour Cream Rice 57
Southern Hash 57
Southern-Style Honey Rice 61
Spanish Rice With Avocado 60
Spicy Chicken Rice Bake 57
Stuffed Bell Peppers 54
Sweet and Sour Chicken 55
Wild Herbed Rice 59
Wild Rice Amandine Casserole 63